YORK NOTES

A Streetcar Named Desire

Tennessee Williams

Notes by Hana Sambrook

Longman   York Press

ACKNOWLEDGEMENTS

We are grateful to The University of the South, Sewanee, Tennessee and New Directions Publishing Corp. for permission to reproduce extracts from *A Streetcar Named Desire* by Tennessee Williams. Copyright © 1947, 1953 by Tennessee Williams, renewed 1975, 1981 The University of the South. All rights whatsoever in this play are strictly reserved and application for performance etc., must be made before rehearsal to Casarotto Ramsay Ltd, National House, 60–66 Wardour Street, London W1V 4ND. No performance may be given unless a licence has been obtained.

The right of Hana Sambrook to be identified as Author of this Work has been asserted by him in accordance with the Copyright, Designs and Patents Act 1988

YORK PRESS
322 Old Brompton Road, London SW5 9JH

PEARSON EDUCATION LIMITED
Edinburgh Gate, Harlow,
Essex CM20 2JE, United Kingdom
Associated companies, branches and representatives throughout the world

© Librairie du Liban *Publishers* and Addison Wesley Longman Limited 1998

First published 1998
Third impression 2000

ISBN 0-582-32930-2

Designed by Vicki Pacey, Trojan Horse, London
Phototypeset by Gem Graphics, Trenance, Mawgan Porth, Cornwall
Colour reproduction and film output by Spectrum Colour
Produced by Pearson Education China Limited, Hong Kong

C ONTENTS

Part one

Introduction

How to study a play

Studying on your own requires self-discipline and a carefully thought-out work plan in order to be effective.

- Drama is a special kind of writing (the technical term is 'genre') because it needs a performance in the theatre to arrive at a full interpretation of its meaning. Try to imagine that you are a member of the audience when reading the play. Think about how it could be presented on the stage, not just about the words on the page.

- Drama is always about conflict of some sort (which may be below the surface). Identify the conflicts in the play and you will be close to identifying the large ideas or themes which bind all the parts together.

- Make careful notes on themes, character, plot and any sub-plots of the play.

- Why do you like or dislike the characters in the play? How do your feelings towards them develop and change?

- Playwrights find non-realistic ways of allowing an audience to see into the minds and motives of their characters, for example soliloquy, aside or music. Consider how such dramatic devices are used in the play you are studying.

- Think of the playwright writing the play. Why were these particular arrangements of events, characters and speeches chosen?

- Cite exact sources for all quotations, whether from the text itself or from critical commentaries. Wherever possible find your own examples from the play to back up your opinions.

- Always express your ideas in your own words.

This York Note offers an introduction to *A Streetcar Named Desire* and cannot substitute for close reading of the text and the study of secondary sources.

Reading the text of a play as a piece of literary work will always raise the question: to what extent is a play written to be read instead of being performed on the stage?

What are the advantages and disadvantages of what we might call the literary approach? The readers of a play must use their imagination to flesh out the characters, and to place them in an appropriate setting. There is a good deal of satisfaction in doing this. The readers can go back and reread a scene that has caught their imagination or has presented a problem of interpretation.

There need be no break in their reading (no interval for the sale of ice-cream!), and they can give full weight to the significance of the author's use of the conventional division of a play into Acts and scenes. Thus Tennessee Williams divides *A Streetcar Named Desire* into eleven short scenes, not Acts (see Dramatic Technique on Structure on this peculiarity of the play).

Another advantage of reading a play is of course its ready availability in book form. Years may pass before a piece of theatre can be seen on the stage. We should bear in mind, however, that most plays are written for the stage, that the playwrights expect their work to be seen and *heard* (this too is important) by an audience in the theatre.

Of course there have been plays written expressly to be read, which the author never intended for the stage. Labelled **closet drama**, such plays include John Milton's *Samson Agonistes* (1671), Percy Bysshe Shelley's *Prometheus Unbound* (1820) and *The Cenci* (1819), William Wordsworth's *The Borderers* (1842), and, in the twentieth century and in another medium, Dylan Thomas's scenario for a film about the Edinburgh body-snatchers, entitled *The Doctor and the Devils* (1953). Certainly, there have been stage performances of such plays (some years ago *Samson Agonistes* was staged during the Edinburgh Festival), but the author's intention was primarily to write a poem to be read rather than performed.

Tennessee Williams wrote his plays for the stage and was eager to see them performed. Yet his stage directions often go far beyond practical instructions and can only be fully appreciated when reading the play. Thus in the description of Elysian Fields at the start of Scene 1 he speaks of the evening sky that '*gracefully attenuates the atmosphere of decay*'. When Blanche Dubois arrives on the scene, the description of her unsuitably dainty dress ends with the ominous words '*There is something about her uncertain manner ... that suggests a moth*, words that hint at her fragility and her helplessness, and foreshadow her tragic end.

Did Tennessee Williams expect his plays to be read? Was that why he paid as much attention to the wording of the stage directions as to the words spoken by the characters in the play? Or is it simply that a writer like Tennessee Williams found **metaphors** the most accurate means of conveying what he expected to see on the stage? The use of language in *A Streetcar Named Desire* will be discussed later (see Language and Style), yet it is useful for the readers to be aware of some aspects of his work when starting to read his play.

A stage performance will, to some extent, blot out the characters the readers have created in their imagination. Anyone who has seen Vivien Leigh and Marlon Brando as Blanche and Stanley in the 1951 film version of *A Streetcar Named Desire* will find their powerful screen presences difficult to dismiss.

When reading a play we become more fully aware of its literary aspects. On the stage the words spoken by the actors serve to create tension, to move the action forward, and as spectators all we are aware of is how convincing and compelling the actors' words are. During our reading of the play we can appreciate the beauty of the language as much as its dramatic effectiveness. We have time too to think of parallels and echoes which will add to our understanding of the play. The sexual tension between Blanche and Stanley, heightened by class differences, may bring to mind D.H. Lawrence's Lady Chatterley and the gamekeeper Mellors in the 1928 novel *Lady Chatterley's Lover*, or August Strindberg's Miss Julie and the footman Jean in the play *Miss Julie* (1888). Such parallels serve to underline the play's violent and tragic ending.

When reading the play we can also consider its autobiographical element. Tennessee Williams himself was aware of the importance of this. He said: 'I must find characters who correspond to my own tensions' (quoted in *Tennessee Williams: Rebellious Puritan* by Nancy Tischler, p. 246). *A Streetcar Named Desire* is not so closely based on Tennessee Williams's own experiences as his *The Glass Menagerie*, but there are aspects of the play that reflect his own story. A man who had been nicknamed Tennessee (see Background) was certainly as aware of his Southern-ness as his Blanche was. Blanche's betrayal by her own sister which results in her committal to a mental hospital is a parallel of Tennessee Williams's own guilt-ridden feelings about his sister Rose who was lobotomised during his absence at university, and sent to a state mental hospital.

Finally, reading about Blanche's promiscuity, hinted at by her flirtatious manner and cruelly exposed by Stanley, we may well remember Tennessee Williams's own homosexual liaisons. It has been suggested that, in creating Blanche, Tennessee Williams was indulging in imaginative cross-dressing, that he wrote of a promiscuous heterosexual woman because homosexuality was then still illegal in most American states. However we view this possibility, we can appreciate that the title of the play, *A Streetcar Named Desire*, conveys Tennessee Williams's view of any sexual passion as an inexorable force that will take its victim along a path to self-destruction that is as unbending as the tracks of a streetcar.

Obviously such speculations are not possible for the audience in a theatre, carried along by the speed of the action and by their own immediate reactions. Thinking and talking about the performance later will often touch on topics that come to mind during the reading of a play. It is arguable of course that speculation about the autobiographical aspects of a play or its literary antecedents is in the last resort irrelevant: the play's the thing.

Yet any thoughts that increase our interest in the play and widen our perception of it are valuable and enriching. It is hoped that this Note will stimulate the readers' interest in the play by encouraging them to consider the questions it raises.

The first reading of *A Streetcar Named Desire* should be for the pleasure of discovering what the play is about. When rereading the play the students should move beyond the simple storyline to a more critical approach. The questions touched on here, as well as other aspects of the play, will be discussed in the following pages.

Part two

Summaries

Tennessee Williams started work on *A Streetcar Named Desire* in 1945.
Early in the year he wrote the first version, entitled 'The Moth' (evidently
the metaphor of Blanche as a delicate, doomed moth caught his imagination quite early on). He then put the play aside, returning to it a little later
in the same year.

He named this second version 'Blanche's Chair in the Moon' –
Blanche took centre stage again. By the summer of 1945 the play was given
another title again, 'The Poker Night'. As the title implies, the play no
longer centres on Blanche alone. The poker players of Scenes 3 and 11 of
the final version of the play now take up their places, their comments on
the game providing a counterpoint to Blanche's fantasies.

The changes in the title indicate a shift of emphasis in the play, but
there were other changes as well. To begin with, the family at the centre of
the play was Italian, but later the brother-in-law became an Irishman and
the two sisters turned into Southern belles. Later again the brother-in-law
became a Polish-American. Most of the Polish immigrants before the
1940s and 1950s were not political refugees, or middle class – they were
labourers, mostly uneducated and looked down upon. The change was
made to emphasise the class element in the play which adds another
dimension to the sexual tension between Blanche and Stanley.

The play was first published in New York by New Directions in 1947.
It was reissued, with an introduction by Tennessee Williams, by New
American Library, New York, in 1951. By this time the play had been
successfully staged in New York. An acting edition was published by the
Dramatists' Play Service, New York, in 1953.

In Britain *A Streetcar Named Desire* was first published in London in
1949 by John Lehmann, and reissued in 1956 by Secker & Warburg,
London, in a collection entitled *Four Plays*. A paperback edition in one
volume with *The Glass Menagerie* appeared under the Penguin imprint in
1959 in their Penguin Plays series. A volume entitled *A Streetcar Named
Desire and Other Plays* (containing *A Streetcar Named Desire*, *Sweet Bird of*

Youth and *The Glass Menagerie*) was published in the Penguin Twentieth-Century Classics in 1962.

In 1984 a Methuen Student Edition of the play was published, with notes by Patricia Hern, and with stills from the 1951 film version of the play. This edition was used in the preparation of these notes.

Readers might also be interested in the stage history of *A Streetcar Named Desire*. It was first performed in the United States in November 1947 in Boston under the direction of Elia Kazan, and in December of the same year in New York. Jessica Tandy played Blanche and Marlon Brando took the part of Stanley. Later Blanche was played in turn by Uta Hagen and Tallulah Bankhead (herself a Southerner from Alabama) while Brando was replaced for a time by Anthony Quinn.

The British première was in 1949 at the Aldwych Theatre in London under the direction of Laurence Olivier. Vivien Leigh played Blanche and Bonar Colleano played Stanley. In 1951 a film version of the play was made, directed by Elia Kazan. Vivien Leigh and Marlon Brando played the leading parts to considerable acclaim.

Synopsis

The play opens on a May evening outside a shabby house in a rundown street in New Orleans, grandly named Elysian Fields. The house belongs to Eunice and Steve Hubbel, and Stanley and Stella Kowalski rent an apartment there.

Eunice is sitting on the steps of the house with a black neighbour when an incongruously dainty woman comes round the corner, carrying a suitcase. She is Stella Kowalski's older sister, Blanche Dubois, arriving on a visit. She accepts Eunice's invitation to wait for Stella in the Kowalskis' apartment.

Stella returns and though the sisters embrace affectionately, an underlying tension makes itself felt. Blanche seems on the defensive, having sold *lost* the family property, Belle Reve. The circumstances of the sale are never fully explained. *IT WAS MORTGAGED TO RAISE LOANS & LOST ON DEFAULT OF PAYMENT*

When Stanley returns home he accepts Blanche's presence quite amiably, but it soon becomes obvious that her genteel pretensions will clash with his macho self-confidence. Through his questioning of Blanche we learn that she had been married and that her husband is dead.

The next evening (Scene 2) Stanley's friends Mitch, Steve and Pablo are coming to play poker, and Stella decides to take her sister out for the evening. Stanley resents the arrangement and, when Stella tells him of the loss of Belle Reve, he suspects that Stella, and he with her, has been cheated by her sister out of her rightful share of the sale.

He pulls out Blanche's large trunk and accusingly displays all her finery as her spoils of the sale. When Blanche comes in after her bath, she flirts with him, but her flirtatious, playful manner arouses his suspicions in another way. Though uneducated, he is no fool, and he realises that his sister-in-law is behaving like a streetwalker. He demands to see the legal papers concerning the sale, explaining that Stella is pregnant which makes him all the more anxious about his rights.

Much later the same evening (Scene 3) when the sisters return from their evening out, the poker game is still in progress. Stanley has been drinking and he resents Blanche's interest in one of the players, the shy Mitch, a bachelor.

There is a violent scene, and Stanley hits his wife. The hysterical Blanche takes her sister up to Eunice's flat, but later she is shocked to find that Stella has gone back to her husband and is in bed with him.

The next day (Scene 4) Stella makes it clear to her sister that she loves her husband and has no intention of leaving him in spite of his brutality. Stanley overhears Blanche's condemnation of him.

Spurred on by his resentment of Blanche (Scene 5) Stanley makes enquiries about her and discovers that she was forced to leave Laurel, her home town, because of her reckless promiscuity. His hints about her past terrify Blanche, and she tries to explain to her sister her past behaviour and her terror of growing old. She admits that she is hoping to marry Mitch, and Stella encourages her hopes. Waiting for Mitch, Blanche flirts recklessly with a young subscription collector.

Blanche's evening out with Mitch is not a success (Scene 6). Mitch is painfully aware of his dullness. He comes in for a nightcap, and to begin with they converse awkwardly. Gradually they begin to talk more seriously, Mitch about his ailing mother and Blanche about her husband's suicide after she had found him in bed with another man. Moved by her tragic story, Mitch takes her in his arms.

It is now September (Scene 7), and it is Blanche's birthday. A birthday dinner is planned to which Mitch has been invited. Stella is decorating the birthday cake when Stanley comes in triumphantly with full details of Blanche's scandalous past. Stella refuses to believe all the stories about her sister and is appalled to learn that Stanley has told Mitch everything. Blanche emerges from the bathroom in high spirits, but she soon senses that something is wrong.

Less than an hour later (Scene 8) the dismal dinner is over. Blanche tries in vain to ring Mitch and is growing more and more frightened. Stanley has a birthday present for her – a bus ticket back to Laurel. Stella reproaches him for his cruelty, but stops abruptly. Her labour pains have started.

Left alone in the apartment (Scene 9) Blanche has been drinking. Mitch arrives, unshaven and a little drunk. Blanche is overwhelmed to see him, but soon realises that his attitude towards her has changed. He accuses her of having lied to him about her age and about her past. While admitting what she had done Blanche tries to explain the reasons for her behaviour. Mitch has no desire to understand her, and to show his contempt for her he tries to rape her. Her wild cries frighten him and he runs off.

Alone once more (Scene 10) Blanche goes on drinking steadily. Befuddled by drink and confused by her own fantasies, she dresses up in her tawdry finery while trying to pack her trunk.

Stanley arrives, a little drunk, having been sent home by the hospital as the baby is not expected to arrive before morning. He mocks Blanche's fabrications about a cruise with a rich admirer and about Mitch's penitent return. There is tension between them and Blanche is frightened. Her terror arouses Stanley and he carries her off to the bedroom to rape her.

Some weeks pass (Scene 11) and once more Stanley and his friends are playing poker. Except for Stanley none of the men has much heart for the game. Blanche is heard off-stage, having a bath, while Stella is busy packing her sister's trunk. Eunice comes in and from her conversation with Stella we learn that Stella has arranged for her sister to leave. Stella explains that she cannot believe Blanche's story and go on living with her husband. Blanche believes that she is going on holiday with her old admirer.

A doctor and a matron from a mental hospital arrive. Blanche is frightened and tries to run away, but the matron grabs her and holds her. The doctor's calm, courteous manner calms her and she leaves on his arm.

The sobbing Stella is given her child to hold and, soothed by Stanley's caresses, she yields to his lovemaking.

SCENE 1   Blanche's arrival in Elysian Fields. There is an undercurrent of tension in the meeting between Blanche and Stella. Blanche admits the loss of Belle Reve. An uneasy meeting between Blanche and Stanley

On a May evening in a rundown quarter of New Orleans, in a street ironically named the Elysian Fields, two women, one white and one black, are sitting on the steps of the shabby corner house, enjoying the evening air. The white woman is Eunice who, with her husband Steve, owns the house. Stanley and Stella Kowalski rent an apartment there.

Two men come round the corner – Stanley Kowalski and his friend Mitch. Stanley bellows to his wife that he is on his way to the bowling alley. Stella promises to follow.

As the men leave, a daintily dressed woman appears, carrying a suitcase. She is Blanche Dubois, Stella's elder sister, arriving on a visit. Eunice invites Blanche to wait in the Kowalskis' apartment while the black neighbour fetches Stella. When Stella arrives, the sisters embrace but underlying tensions soon make themselves felt.

Stanley comes in and greets Blanche amicably enough. An uneasy conversation follows, dominated by Stanley's self-assurance. Blanche tells him about the death of her husband some years ago.

The first scene introduces several themes that will dominate the play. Quite early on we are made aware of Blanche's craving for drink. We also realise that her drinking does not go unnoticed either by her sister or by her brother-in-law. In a play the point is stressed by repetitive action while in a novel it might be made by the **authorial voice**.

Also manifest is Blanche's awareness of social distinctions which shows itself in the offhand manner in which she accepts both Eunice's and her neighbour's acts of kindness. To Blanche these are services naturally expected of her social inferiors.

Another aspect of her character revealed in this scene is her vanity and her need of flattery. There is pathos in this: Blanche is afraid of growing old and losing her looks, and needs flattery to banish her terrors. Appealing in her vulnerability she is nevertheless very much the older sister, treating Stella as a child and expecting her to run errands.

Our attention is drawn immediately to Blanche – the greater part of the scene is devoted to building up her character by showing her actions and her reactions to the other characters (see Dramatic Technique on Focus).

Stanley of course also makes an impact: though we do not see much of him in this scene, Tennessee Williams sketches a portrait of him in stage directions that stress the sexual magnetism of this '*gaudy seed-bearer*', explaining Stella's infatuation.

But what of Stella herself? How much do we learn about her beyond what we learn from her words and actions? Her part in the play is by no means insignificant, yet the introductory stage directions offer no description beyond '*a gentle young woman*'. The spectators will see the actress on the stage but the readers of the play must use their imagination and start to piece together a picture of Stella.

Two themes introduced in Scene 1 cannot be fully appreciated by those who read the play rather than attending a performance. The 'blue piano' and the polka are heard now, and will be heard repeatedly throughout the play. The readers of course have only Tennessee Williams's descriptions of the music to guide them, yet perhaps the presence of stage directions stresses the importance of the music more. The audience in a theatre, concentrating on the action, may not pay much attention to background music. After all, we are all used to music in films, and have perhaps learnt to disregard it, though it may still affect our feelings about what we are watching.

There is another way in which the readers benefit from the stage directions. Tennessee Williams's directions are evocative, precise in their use of **imagery** and inevitably stand in contrast to the language used by most of the characters on the stage, with the exception of Blanche and Stella. They serve to underline the uneducated speech of most of the people on the stage.

Elysian Fields in classical mythology this is the equivalent of paradise, the place where those favoured by the gods go after death. There is obvious irony in the choice of this name for a rundown street, but we should also remember that the Elysian Fields were the dwelling-place of the dead. Blanche's ultimate fate will be the living death of the asylum

L & N tracks the tracks of the Louisiana & Nashville railroad

'Blue piano' though Tennessee Williams's note describes it as expressing the spirit of the place, this music goes beyond giving a touch of local colour, and its message changes throughout the play

poor boy's sandwich French loaf split and filled with slices of meat

suggests a moth a hint at Blanche's fragility; we may remember that an earlier version of the play was entitled 'The Moth'

a street-car named Desire Tennessee Williams had actually seen in New Orleans a streetcar (tram) with this curious destination. Here it is used ironically; equally, however, it might be seen as a metaphor for the driving force of sexual desire (see Imagery and Symbolism)

the ghoul-haunted woodland of Weir a quotation from Edgar Allan Poe's poem 'Ulalumé'. The literary reference reminds us that Blanche is a schoolteacher

Belle Reve the Dubois family home. Belle Reve means 'beautiful dream'

Polacks contemptuous American term for people of Polish origin

is Mass out yet a coarse joke depending on the similarity of pronunciation between 'Mass' and 'my ass' (US for 'my backside')

The music of the polka the second musical theme of the play. Its function is more clearly defined than that of the blue piano: Blanche hears the polka when she remembers her dead husband

SCENE 2   **The sisters prepare for an evening out. Stanley's fury at the loss of Belle Reve. Blanche flirts with Stanley. She learns that her sister is pregnant**

The following evening Blanche and Stella are getting ready for an evening out while Stanley is playing poker with his friends. He is clearly annoyed at being left behind. When Stella tells him that Belle Reve is lost, he wants to know how the house was disposed of. He believes that under Louisiana law any property belonging to his wife also belongs to him and he believes that he has been robbed. Furious, he pulls open Blanche's large trunk and displays all her finery which he believes to be genuine, costly items bought with money that should have been his. Stella is angry and rushes out.

At this point Blanche comes in, radiant after a long bath. While getting ready she flirts with Stanley, but he refuses to pay her the compliments she expects. He demands to see the papers relating to the sale of Belle Reve, and pulls open her trunk to look for them. To Blanche's distress he finds the letters from her dead husband. On being presented with a strongbox of papers he seems a little ashamed and explains that any inheritance would be important because Stella is expecting a baby.

Stella comes in and the sisters embrace. As they set out, Stanley's friends arrive.

> In this scene Stanley's antagonism to Blanche grows, as do his suspicions about her. Both the motive and the means for her destruction are now becoming clear, as the playwright prepares the ground for the inevitable calamity.

> Stanley's hostility is rooted in his sharp awareness of the class differences between himself and Blanche (and by implication his wife as well), and his instinctive reaction is to pull her down to his level. The sexual implications are obvious: his sexuality is his means of domination. Later on, in Scene 8, he says this to Stella quite explicitly ('I pulled you down off them columns [of Belle Reve] and how you loved it').

> This class antagonism is intensified by Stanley's suspicions that he has been cheated by the smart-talking Blanche. When he pulls out all Blanche's clothes and jewellery he betrays his ignorance of the true value of the articles. Again he is at a loss and his resentment grows because his wife mocks him.

> Tennessee Williams has divided the scene into two parts: first we have Stella instructing her husband how to treat the highly strung visitor, and telling him of the loss of Belle Reve. Already resentful, Stanley explodes in anger at being swindled, and grows angrier still when his wife laughs at him for overestimating the value of Blanche's wardrobe.

> When Stella rushes off angrily, the second part of the scene begins with Blanche making an appearance in her red robe. Blind to Stanley's rage she postures flirtatiously. Her manner is such that it

arouses Stanley's suspicions in another direction. He is experienced and shrewd enough to sense that his sister-in-law's provocative behaviour is more fitting for a prostitute than for a schoolteacher. He now begins to wonder about her past ('If I didn't know that you was my wife's sister I'd get ideas about you!').

This then might be seen as the main function of the scene – to set the tragedy in motion. The warning signals would be picked up easily by the audience in the theatre, especially in the second half, with Stanley's smouldering rage set against Blanche's misguided playfulness. The readers of the play are guided by Tennessee Williams's stage directions and the printed text of the dialogues – and their own imagination.

A new motif is introduced in this scene and will recur again and again: Blanche's habit of taking long baths. On a purely practical level, this habit is obviously very irritating to the other occupants of the apartment and will increase the tension significantly. As so often with Tennessee Williams, however, there is a symbolic aspect to this obsessive habit (the role of such symbols will be discussed more fully later in Imagery and Symbolism). What starts here as a selfish obsessive habit will become a pathetic act of contrition. Like the 'blue piano' the motif will return, with different meanings.

the perpetual "blue piano" the perfunctory reference to the music seems at this point to relegate it to a background accompaniment

the Napoleonic code the Code Napoléon, a code of laws compiled at the instigation of Napoleon I in 1800–1804, which is still the base of French law today. Louisiana had been a French colony, under the French law, but it was sold to the United States in 1803, so that the Code Napoléon was never really in operation there. Stanley seems nevertheless obsessed by his notion of the Code

The first anniversary gift a reference to the first wedding anniversary, traditionally called a paper anniversary

The "blue piano" sounds louder here the music stresses an important piece of news

Red hots! the tamale vendor's cry. It startles Blanche, perhaps as a reminder of sexual passion, and of her past

SCENE 2 continued

The blind are – leading the blind a proverb from Matthew 15:14, used by Jesus about the Pharisees: 'And if the blind lead the blind, both shall fall into the ditch.' The implication here seems to be one of impending disaster

Then the "blue piano" and the hot trumpet sound louder perhaps the vitality of the quarter triumphing over Blanche's forebodings

SCENE 3
The sisters return. The poker game is still on. Stanley is drunk and resentful of Mitch's interest in Blanche. A violent row erupts and Stanley hits Stella. She is taken to Eunice's apartment by the hysterical Blanche, but returns to her husband. Blanche is shocked; Mitch comforts her

Much later that night the men are still playing poker. The sisters return and Blanche is snubbed by Stanley for her genteel airs. She shows interest in the shy Mitch, especially noting that he is not married.

As the sisters talk, Stanley orders them to be quiet and turns off Blanche's radio. She turns it on again and Stanley throws it out of the window. Stella rushes at him, and he hits her.

His friends hold him, speaking gently to him, but Blanche runs in hysterically to collect Stella's clothes. Both sisters go upstairs, intending to sleep in Eunice's apartment.

Stanley sobers up and shouts for his wife. Stella appears and they embrace passionately. Blanche is appalled to find that her sister has gone back to her husband. Mitch comforts her, explaining that the Kowalskis are 'crazy about each other'. His soft voice calms Blanche, and they sit on the steps talking.

In this scene the relations between the main characters are clarified further. It is one of the pivotal scenes of the play. That Tennessee Williams thought of it in this way is indicated by his choice of the title 'The Poker Party' for the third version of the play.

The dramatic purpose of the poker party is to demonstrate Stanley's domination over his friends through the way in which he makes all the decisions about the game. The scene shows also their devotion to him through their tender handling of him when he is drunk.

Particularly important for the plot is the relationship between Mitch and Stanley. That the latter is jealous of Mitch's interest in Blanche is made clear by his calling Mitch back to the poker game and particularly by the fact that he is watching Mitch ('He was looking through them drapes' – at Blanche). The sequence of cause and effect is to be traced also in Stanley's drunken rage when he hits Stella. That she returns to him that same night is further proof of the strength of her passion in which his violent behaviour plays a part. Blanche's hysterical determination to take Stella away from her husband (which continues into the next scene) is not forgotten or forgiven by Stanley, and makes him all the more determined to be rid of the unwelcome visitor.

In this scene we also learn more about Blanche: her vanity betrays her into the foolish lie about Stella's age, and the equally foolish claim that she has come in order to help out as her sister has not been well.

Blanche's seductive posturing half-undressed in the gap between the curtains to the bedroom will be remembered when Stanley reveals her promiscuous past (Scene 7). To her such behaviour is instinctive when there are men around. Her behaviour underlines the contradictions in her character, the genteel Southern lady who expects men to stand up when she comes in and who cannot bear a rude remark or a vulgar action, and the cheap seductress.

Worth noting are Blanche's words to Mitch at the close of the scene, 'I need kindness now'; moving in their honesty, they will be recalled in the last scene when she says to the doctor: 'I have always depended on the kindness of strangers'. The words are the author's appeal on her behalf for the audience to understand and pity her.

One-eyed jacks knaves of spades and hearts
wild having a value to be decided on by the players
Ante up! let's play for higher stakes!
Openers opening bids
Spade flush a hand of cards consisting of spades only
Seven card stud a variety of poker
Please don't get up courtesy to women was a part of the Southern social code
Xavier Cougat a popular American band leader of the Thirties and Forties
Spit in the Ocean a type of poker game
Little Boys' Room a coy euphemism for a lavatory

my favourite sonnet this is Sonnet 43 from *Sonnets from the Portuguese* (1850) by Elizabeth Barrett Browning (1806–61). We are reminded here that Blanche taught English at Laurel

Wien, Wien, nur du allein 'Vienna, Vienna, only you', title of a Viennese waltz

All quiet on the Potomac a catchphrase dating back to the American Civil War (1861–5). It is usually attributed to General George McClellan who pushed the Southern Confederate army back over the river Potomac in 1862

SCENE 4   **Stella is still in bed. Blanche appeals to her to leave Stanley. Stella refuses. Stanley overhears Blanche's condemnation of him**

The following morning Stella is still in bed, alone, peaceful and happy. Blanche rushes in, hysterical after a sleepless night. She reproaches her sister for going back to her husband and sleeping with him.

Stella explains calmly that Stanley is always violent when drunk and that he is now ashamed of himself. Her calm acceptance outrages Blanche. She wants to leave, taking Stella with her. She listens in disbelief when Stella tells her that she loves her husband and will not leave him.

To Blanche Stanley is a brute, and while she tells Stella this, Stanley approaches unseen and hears it all. He withdraws and returns noisily, calling for his wife. They embrace and Stanley grins triumphantly at Blanche over Stella's head.

Though this scene seems at first to provide an interval of calm, the tensions quickly build up. Blanche fails to understand Stella's passionate relationship with her husband. It seems that with all her sexual experience (of which we learn in Scene 7) Blanche has never experienced true passion. Stella has no patience with Blanche's hysterical plans, and her irritation shows in her dry ironical comments. She starts to resent her sister's disapproval and harsh criticism of Stanley. Will this play a part in her decision in the last scene?

As well as telling us more about the sisters, the scene also has a dramatic function. Having overheard Blanche's melodramatic condemnation of himself as a brute, an ape-man, Stanley now has even more reason to dislike Blanche and to wish to find a way of getting rid of her. His triumphant grin at the close of the scene promises ill for Blanche.

a book of coloured comics Stella's choice of reading testifies that she has joined a world in which comics are read, not books

wore his pin a member of a college fraternity (undergraduates' elite society) gave his fraternity pin to his girlfriend to wear, to show that she was his girl

Western Union one of the largest telephone companies in the United States

bromo tranquillising headache pill

It brought me here Blanche's remark can mean simply that the streetcar to Desire brought her to her sister's house. Equally it is a metaphor for the sexual desire that has ruined her life and brought her to New Orleans to live on her sister's charity

someone to go out with Blanche means rather more than that – a man to go to bed with. The remark is of some importance as it is unusual for Blanche to admit, however obliquely, that she knows about sexual relationships

Bringing the raw meat home Blanche unwittingly recalls Stanley's bloodstained parcel of butcher's meat in Scene 1

SCENE 5   **Stanley hints at Blanche's past. She tries to explain to Stella the reasons for her past behaviour, and her fear of growing old. Her hopes to marry Mitch are encouraged by Stella. Blanche flirts with a young man just before Mitch's arrival**

Some time later, a noisy row is heard from the upstairs flat as Eunice accuses Steve of infidelity. She rushes out, with Steve following, while the sisters listen below, amused.

Stanley returns from his bowling, and it is clear from Blanche's nervous behaviour that she is afraid of him, with good reason. He tells her that an acquaintance of his remembers meeting her at a disreputable hotel in the town where she taught. Blanche denies this but looks terrified.

Stanley leaves, and Blanche tries to find out how much her sister knows of her past, and to explain the reasons for her past behaviour. She admits that she is nervous: Mitch is coming to take her out, and she is desperate to attract him because she is afraid of growing old and unattractive, and of being alone.

Stella tries to reassure her as she leaves to join Stanley. A young man calls at the apartment, collecting subscriptions to a paper. Blanche flirts with him, to his embarrassment, and then sends him on his way, just before Mitch arrives with a bunch of red roses.

A threatening undertone runs through this scene. It opens with a violent row between Eunice and Steve which is followed by a hostile interchange between Stanley and Blanche. It is clear that Stanley has discovered something about Blanche's past and that she is frightened.

Blanche's confession to Stella about her fears for the future and her hopes of finding safety with Mitch is harrowing because she now admits, however indirectly, her past liaisons and recognises that they were just a way of asserting her existence.

We pity her and fear for her because we now realise that an instinct for self-destruction will always overpower her, that she will always go astray, propelled by sexual greed. This is made clear by her flirtation with the young collector for a local newspaper. She sends him away but not before she has kissed him, moments before Mitch arrives.

Tennessee Williams uses the brief scene with the young man to show the contradictions in Blanche's character. She is desperate to marry Mitch, yet she is ready to risk her future in this flirtatious episode. Is it an urge to self-destruction? Or is it that she has no real desire for the safety of married life because in her heart she cannot commit herself to a permanent relationship with one man? The moth will flutter and not settle down. Tennessee Williams clearly intends to arouse doubts about Blanche, hence this curious episode which puts at risk the material and emotional security she desires.

Dramatically this episode does more than make us doubt Blanche's real desires. For most readers – or spectators – there is now no possibility of a happy ending for this wretched woman. The question now remains only when and how the blow will fall.

lots of banging around the double meaning (acting noisily; having sexual intercourse) is intentional
Not in front of your sister Stanley's refusal to kiss his wife in Blanche's presence betrays his sexual awareness of her
the colours of butterfly wings recalls the metaphor of Blanche as a moth in Scene 1

put a – **paper lantern over the light** a metaphor for Blanche's need to
camouflage unpleasant reality (for Blanche's explanation of her purchase see
Scene 3; for the symbolic meaning of the paper lantern see Imagery and
Symbolism)
a piercing cry perhaps the dark stain on the white skirt reminds Blanche of
blood, of her husband's suicide
'put out' make blatant use of her physical attractions
You make my mouth water there is a sexual undertone in this
keep my hands off children a hint at the scandal that put an end to Blanche's
teaching career
Rosenkavalier 'the knight of the rose', the eponymous hero of Richard
Strauss's opera (1911)

SCENE 6 The evening out with Mitch has been a failure. Back at
the apartment Blanche and Mitch talk awkwardly at first.
Later Blanche tells him of her husband's suicide. Mitch
embraces her, suggesting marriage

Well after midnight Mitch and Blanche return. The evening has not been
a success, and Mitch feels he has been dull. Blanche invites him in for a
nightcap. At first the conversation remains awkward in spite of Blanche's
feverish attempts at gaiety. Then they begin to talk more seriously, Mitch
of his ailing mother, Blanche of the suicide of her husband after she had
found him in bed with another man. Mitch, deeply moved, embraces her
as she weeps.

The opening mood of this scene is downbeat and depressing; the
evening out has been a failure, and both Mitch and Blanche know it,
and are dispirited by their inadequacies.

While Mitch apologises for his dullness, Blanche's reaction is to be
feverishly gay, pretending to the incomprehending Mitch that they
are in a café on the Left Bank in Paris. Her desperate attempt is of
course doomed to failure, and stresses her inability to understand
other people, isolated as she is in the world of her imagination.

Her play-acting is a prelude to a dramatic change of mood when she
and Mitch talk seriously. It has another purpose as well: to stress her
need for make-believe situations which make it possible for her to

bear her blighted life. Indeed it might be said that Blanche is almost incapable of facing reality – not only its uglier aspects, but its humdrum ordinary demands as well. She sees Mitch as her salvation, but could she bear the life of the wife of a factory worker?

There are moments in this scene that hint at her unwillingness to go on with the play-acting inherent in her relationship with Mitch. While pretending to be in a Paris café she bluntly offers to sleep with him, certain that he does not understand French. Again, when speaking to him of her old-fashioned ideas about women's behaviour, she rolls her eyes self-mockingly, knowing that he cannot see her face.

On both these occasions she risks being found out by Mitch. As in the episode with the young man in the preceding scene she recklessly endangers her hard-won position with Mitch, as if in her heart she wished to make sure that for her there never would be the dull safety of marriage. And yet at the close of the scene her humble gratitude is sincere. It puzzles us yet engages our sympathy.

Also worth noting here is the significance of Blanche's incoherent musing about Stanley's dislike of her. Incomprehensible to Mitch, her half-spoken conjecture is that Stanley's dislike of her might be a kind of perverse sexual attraction. Her knowledge of men, gained in all those one-night stands in Laurel, is obvious here though never comprehended by the simple Mitch.

As well as casting light on her past, her speculation foreshadows her fatal encounter with Stanley in Scene 10. The rape that will drive her into her fantasy world for good is foretold here and its motive defined accurately, as will be acknowledged by Stanley in the later scene – 'We've had this date with each other from the beginning!'

The dramatic device of forewarning the spectators or readers of what is going to happen is used here only obliquely. It might pass unnoticed in a stage performance of the play, but will be picked up by students of the printed text who have the leisure to give the words their full weight.

owl-car all-night tramcar
La Dame aux Camellias ... Armand! Marguerite Gautier, a Parisian high-class

call-girl, and her lover Armand whom she renounces, in Alexandre Dumas the Younger's 1848 novel, *La dame aux camélias*

Voulez-vous coucher ... quel dommage! 'would you like to sleep with me tonight? You don't understand? Ah, what a pity!' (probably intentionally Tennessee Williams uses the standard invitation of a French prostitute)

wash-coat (US) light washable jacket

the Varsouviana the Warsaw polka

the Polka resumes in a major key the polka stops at the moment of her husband's death and resumes in a major key to emphasise the impact of the dreadful memory

Sometimes – there's God – so quickly! as in Scenes 2 and 3 Blanche's words sum up the climax obliquely with dramatic effect

SCENE 7   **Stella is preparing Blanche's birthday dinner. Mitch has been invited. Stanley arrives triumphantly with details of Blanche's promiscuous past. Mitch has been told and will not be coming**

It is now September, and it is Blanche's birthday. While she is taking a bath, Stella is putting the final touches to the birthday cake. Stanley comes in triumphantly with details of Blanche's scandalous past. She had been promiscuous even while still living at Belle Reve, meeting drunken soldiers at night. When the house was sold she moved to a cheap hotel with a bad reputation, but the management asked her to leave because of her scandalous behaviour. She was dismissed from her teaching post for seducing one of the pupils.

Stella refuses to accept all of this as true, while admitting that Blanche's flighty behaviour had caused concern at home. She blames Blanche's disastrous early marriage and her husband's suicide for it.

She is appalled to learn that Stanley has told Mitch about Blanche's past, thus putting an end to Blanche's hopes of marrying Mitch. When Blanche emerges from the bathroom she realises at once that something has happened and she is frightened.

This is a short scene full of dramatic contrasts. The cheerful mood of pleasant anticipation (Blanche singing in her bath; Stella arranging the birthday table) is shattered when the triumphant Stanley comes in with the full details of Blanche's past. His convincing account of

SCENE 7 continued

Blanche's shocking behaviour is constantly contrasted with her sentimental song off-stage.

The full dramatic impact of the scene relies not on the details of Blanche's past, shocking as they are, but on her ignorance of what is happening outside the bathroom. Her bathing, on one level a **metaphor** for her yearning to be rid of her past (see Imagery and Symbolism), provides an opportunity in this scene to contrast Stanley's revelations with her ignorance of them. Her blithe singing in the bath, almost within earshot of Stanley's account, plays an important part in raising the tension.

That Tennessee Williams planned this is evident in his use of the word 'contrapuntally' in the stage directions. The use of two speakers, one commenting on the other, usually in derogatory terms, is not original; it is employed, for instance, in Shakespeare's *Henry IV, Part II* (1597), Act II, Scene 4, where the Prince and Poins listen to Falstaff slandering them to Doll, and make furious comments on what they hear. Tennessee Williams makes use of a familiar, often used formula to good effect.

on the nose exactly

contrapuntally as an accompaniment, but in a different, contrasting mood

Barnum and Bailey famous American circus. Here the phrase is used to mean something artificial

loco (US) mad

It's not my soul I'm worried about! a broad hint at Blanche's immorality

degenerate homosexual; homosexuality was considered unacceptable and was illegal, and there was a reluctance to use the word

SCENE 8 **The disastrous birthday party is over. Stanley gives Blanche a cruel birthday present of a bus ticket back to Laurel. A quarrel between Stella and Stanley is interrupted by her labour pains**

Less than an hour later Blanche, Stella and Stanley are finishing the dreadful birthday meal. Blanche is making desperate attempts at conversation, but Stanley remains sullen, reacting with fury to his wife's criticism of his table manners.

Feigning amiability he presents Blanche with a birthday gift – a bus ticket back to Laurel. She rushes off to be sick, and Stella reproaches her husband for his cruelty. Suddenly she stops and asks him to take her to the hospital. Her labour pains have started.

The scene opens with the disastrous birthday dinner. There is tension between the participants who find themselves with nothing to say. The tension is shared by the audience (or readers) who wait for Blanche to learn of the calamity that is about to overwhelm her.

The candle-lighting ceremony offers no respite and is followed by Stanley's brutal birthday present to Blanche of a bus ticket back to Laurel. The scene is brought to an abrupt end by the start of Stella's labour pains.

This is a disjointed scene, with changes of mood from embarrassment to violence, to a pathetic attempt at normality, to Stanley's brutality, ending with Stella's labour pains. For her and Stanley the focus now shifts away from Blanche's distress.

Does Tennessee Williams use the start of Stella's labour as a **deus ex machina** to resolve a difficult situation in the plot? There is certainly an abrupt change of mood, a movement away from Blanche, yet she reclaims our attention in the last moments of the scene. Whether she realises fully her present position or not, she seems different, whispering the repetitive Spanish words in a dazed manner which perhaps foreshadows her descent into unreality.

Of course Stella's labour pains also serve another purpose in the plot. Her departure to the hospital leaves Blanche alone in the apartment for the next two scenes, with tragic results.

Huey Long Huey Pierce Long (1893–1935), governor of Louisiana. A corrupt politician who was nevertheless popular with the voters because he improved the social services and reduced unemployment by a public works programme

get the coloured lights going reach the climax of sexual passion

the Greyhound a long distance coach company

I pulled you down off them columns I brought you down to my level (an interesting comparison may be made here with Strindberg's *Miss Julie* where the footman Jean says to Miss Julie, 'Fall to my level – then I can pick you up again!')

SCENE 8 continued

them coloured lights Stanley used the same metaphor earlier in this scene

El pan de mais maize bread with salt (a Mexican folk song telling how God created man out of maize)

SCENE 9   Blanche is alone, drinking. Mitch arrives, unshaven and drunk. He accuses her of deceit, and when she tries to explain herself, he will not listen. He tries to rape her and is frightened off by her cries

Later that evening Blanche is sitting alone in the apartment, drinking. An unexpected visitor arrives – Mitch. He too has been drinking, and makes it clear that he knows all about Blanche's pretensions to youth and innocence. She tries to explain herself, speaking of her husband's suicide, but Mitch brushes aside her explanations. He tries to make love to her in a manner that shows his contempt for her. Her screams frighten him and he runs off.

This scene marks a decisive stage in Blanche's disintegration. She is drinking heavily and the past, symbolised by the insistent polka music, presses down on her. Mitch's arrival must seem to her like a heaven-sent miracle, and as she rushes about to hide the tell-tale signs of her drinking, she talks feverishly in her excitement.

Her playful manner jars; it is obvious that she is becoming aware of the change in Mitch's behaviour towards her. We sense her despair when Mitch sees in the strong light that she is much older than she had pretended to be. As she lied about her age so she lied about her past, and now she tells Mitch the truth. She admits her many affairs ('many intimacies with strangers') with which she hoped to fill the emptiness of her life.

Mitch, however, is unable to understand what might have driven her to act as she had done. The melodramatic appearance of the Mexican woman selling '*flores para los muertos*' (flowers for the dead) stresses how surrounded by death Blanche had been at Belle Reve.

Yet Blanche's reasons are just so many fancies to Mitch, and he rejects her as unclean, and tries to rape her. Her screams startle him as much as they frighten him. He cannot see why a woman like her can object to sexual advances. His astonishment underlines the total lack of understanding between them, and so, indirectly, the hopelessness of Blanche's earlier efforts to find peace and contentment with him.

The scene works on several levels. For the first time we are given some insights into Blanche's behaviour at Laurel when she tells the truth as she sees it. Against the background of the flower-seller's chant she describes her life at Belle Reve when she maintained the pretence of gracious living for her mother while dealing with the sordid necessities of dying. We also hear a clear declaration of her belief in the truth of the imagination ('I tell what *ought* to be truth', 'I didn't lie in my heart').

She loses the last shreds of hope for peace as Mitch rejects her with contempt. The scene is now set for the inevitable tragedy.

the 'Varsouviana' is heard only the polka music, symbolising her husband's death, is heard until the end of the scene
A distant revolver shot is heard only in Blanche's mind, of course: Mitch hears nothing
boxed out of your mind insane
I don't want realism a plain statement of Blanche's rejection of reality
Flores para los muertos (Spanish) flowers for the dead (there is a strong cult of death in Mexico)
The polka tune fades in the flowers for the dead remind Blanche of her dead husband
blood-stained pillow-slips Blanche is remembering the years when she looked after dying relatives
paddy-wagon police van, Black Maria

SCENE 10   **Blanche dresses up, drunk and half crazy. Stanley returns to wait for the baby's arrival at home. He laughs at Blanche, mocking her illusions. Her terror arouses him and he rapes her**

Blanche has been drinking since Mitch's flight. Dressed in her finery and talking wildly to herself she starts to pack her belongings. Stanley returns from the hospital as the baby is not due yet. He too has been drinking. Blanche invents a story about an invitation to a cruise from a millionaire admirer and adds another about Mitch coming back to beg her to forgive him. Stanley mocks her pretensions, enjoying her evident distress. Finally, he carries her off to the bedroom to rape her.

For Tennessee Williams this scene was the dramatic climax of the play, with the last scene following as a downbeat coda. In Scene 10 he uses every means available to him to create an atmosphere of menace (see Dramatic Technique on Visual and Sound Effects).

The storyline belongs to the realist school of drama, dealing with the downfall of a weak, confused woman against a background of rough low life. In this scene, however (and to some extent in the final scene as well), other elements are introduced to heighten the drama: the background music creates an atmosphere of evil menace, and this atmosphere is underlined by the Expressionist light effects.

There is inherent drama in the spectacle of a half-crazed woman at the end of her tether, dressed up in tawdry finery and acting out her fantasy. It is given full play by the surreal stage effects. The readers of the play are forced to use their imagination to the full, aided by the playwright's copious and detailed stage directions which indicate how much importance he attached to the atmosphere of the scene. Tennessee Williams took considerable risks here by moving away from realism in the stage directions while keeping the dialogue in a realistic key.

Are the *readers* qualified to judge the success of a technique that relies so much on visual and sound effects? (See Dramatic Technique on Visual and Sound Effects for further discussion of this subject.)

honky-tonk music the cheap out-of-tune piano such as is heard in a bar, brings a garish note to the drama to be enacted

A fireman's ball a dance organised by the local fire brigade, a cheap, humble entertainment

his ATO pin his Auxiliary Territorial Officer pin (for the significance of pins in American college life see the notes for Scene 4 above)

Biscayne Boulevard in Miami

a red letter night a special night, a night to celebrate

put on the dog (US) put one one's best clothes

casting my pearls before swine wasting my gifts on people who do not appreciate them (from a biblical phrase in Matthew 7:6, 'neither cast ye your pearls before swine')

Swine, huh? Stanley does not recognise the biblical quotation and thinks that Blanche is insulting him again. Her next remarks confirm his suspicions

Mardi Gras a carnival celebrated in New Orleans on Shrove Tuesday, the day before Ash Wednesday when Lent, the period of fasting, begins

Queen of the Nile Cleopatra, Queen of Egypt (69–30BC)

Lurid reflections appear ... menacing form the stage directions are intended to create a visual image of the nightmare in which Blanche finds herself

The night is filled ... disappear the menacing shapes in Blanche's mind are given a recognisably human form in the sordid incident outside the apartment

rolled robbed while drunk

The inhuman jungle voices rise up the threat of physical violence grows

We've had this date this was meant to happen. Stanley is right, in a way: the tension between them always had sexual overtones. Blanche was always aware of his coarse masculinity, and her provocative behaviour was her reaction to it

SCENE **11**   Some weeks later Stella is packing Blanche's belongings. A subdued poker party is in progress. Blanche expects to be going on a cruise with an admirer but she has been committed to a mental hospital with Stella's approval. The doctor and matron from the hospital arrive. The doctor calms Blanche and she leaves on his arm. Stanley comforts Stella and starts to make love to her

Some weeks have passed. Stella is packing Blanche's belongings while Blanche takes yet another bath. The men are playing poker again but they are all on edge except Stanley. Eunice comes in, and in the course of her conversation with Stella we learn that Stella has arranged for Blanche to leave. Stella explains that quite simply, if she is to go on living with Stanley she must believe that the story of the rape is the invention of a mentally unstable woman.

Blanche thinks that she is going on a cruise with an old admirer; when a doctor and a matron arrive to take her to a mental hospital she is frightened and tries to run away. The matron grabs her but the doctor speaks to her in a kind, courteous manner and she leaves with him quite happily. Stella is distressed but Stanley's caresses soothe her and she yields to his lovemaking.

The final scene starts in a subdued mood. There is a repetition of familiar incidents – Blanche taking a bath, her sister running errands for her, the men playing poker – which emphasises the change of mood.

The mood remains subdued but tension rises: like Blanche, the audience is kept in the dark about what is going to happen. Only gradually do we come to understand that Blanche is going to be committed to a mental hospital. Her sister has given her consent because she cannot go on living with her husband unless she believes that the rape accusation is the fabrication of a crazed mind. No-one condemns Stella for what she has done, except herself, but Blanche goes out at the end without a backward glance at her sister.

After her usual display of vanity and her fussing about her appearance Blanche goes out a curiously dignified figure, saying simply 'Ask her [the matron] to let go of me', and speaking sadly of having to depend on the kindness of strangers. Her ridiculous affectations fall away, and she becomes a truly tragic figure, saluted by the rising men at the poker table.

Ancient Greek tragedy demanded for its main theme the downfall of a great man through his own pride and arrogance (**hubris**). This is not the case here. Blanche Dubois's fall has been a gradual degrading slide, yet at the end she does achieve dignity against all the rules.

It is perhaps the dignity of someone who has nothing, who stands alone, unaware of the fate that awaits her. The effect is to diminish the others in the drama – the sobbing, guilt-stricken Stella, the bragging, bullying Stanley. In dramatic terms it is a stunning **coup de théâtre** which Tennessee Williams pulls off with success.

drew to an inside straight and made it took a risk and was successful
Salerno port in southern Italy, the scene of fierce fighting in the Second World War
Della Robbia blue a vivid blue used by the Italian artist Luca della Robbia (*c.*1400–82) for the background of his reliefs
Are they washed? yet again Blanche's obsessional insistence on cleansing and purity

sewn up in a clean white sack once more the insistence on purity and innocence

Please don't get up we should remember Scene 3 here: this time the men do stand up

Lurid reflections ... noises of the jungle Stanley's presence brings back the memory of the rape. Blanche is now about to undergo another violation – of her mind and of her freedom

The echo sounds ... whispers the sounds and shapes surrounding Blanche convey her panic at being trapped

I have always depended on the kindness of strangers the words remind us of Blanche speaking to Mitch at the close of Scene 3. We now realise the poignant truth that there has been very little kindness in Blanche's life

wrapped in a pale blue blanket the specific stage direction was surely intended to tell us that the baby was a boy, as Stanley so confidently predicted

PART THREE

CRITICAL APPROACHES

CHARACTERISATION

The characterisation in the *text* of a play is quite a different matter from the characterisation in a stage production. When we see a stage performance most of our work is done for us: we see the setting, what the persons in a play look like, and to a considerable extent we are made to see them as the director and the cast conceive them to be. When we read the text of a play, however, we must use our imagination and form our own idea, however nebulous, of the appearance and character of the persons in the play. Here we shall consider how we learn to imagine the action of *A Streetcar Named Desire* on the basis of a simple list of characters and the author's stage directions.

As to the stage directions: readers will have noticed at the start of Scene 1 the detailed description of the stage set, which combines practical details of the appearance of the houses with skilful poetic evocations of the atmosphere ('*the warm breath of the brown river*', the '*peculiarly tender blue*' of the sky). Equally evocative are, for instance, the stage directions at the start of Scene 3.

BLANCHE

To begin with, the characters appearing in Scene 1 are dismissed with only brief description (if any) of their appearance. When Blanche appears, however, she is described in detail, not only her clothes but also the impression she gives of delicacy and vulnerability.

As we read on, her appearance becomes ever clearer and so does her character. Her appearance – slim figure, a face of delicate fading beauty – is described in the stage directions, and the readers also gather further information about her from the other characters' comments. (Indeed she demands flattering comments from her sister, from the reluctant Stanley and from Eunice.)

Her complex, contradictory character also becomes clear. Very early in the play we become aware of her class snobbery (in her dismissal of the black neighbour's kindness and of Eunice's company). We also learn that she is a heavy drinker. The reasons for her craving for alcohol are implied as we learn about her guilt for her husband's suicide and about her promiscuity. Alcohol offers temporary amnesia and reassurance. Equally, her passion for taking long baths should be taken as a symbol of her yearning to wash away her guilt.

We are given the full details of her past later by Stanley, but her cheap seductive manner noted by him with astonishment in Scene 2 and again in Scene 3 is an early warning. As she so primly insists on her respectability to Mitch in Scene 6, readers will inevitably recall her flirting with Stanley earlier as well as the episode with the young man in Scene 5. Here her character is revealed through her actions, leaving the readers to draw their own conclusions.

In her conversation with her sister in Scene 4 Blanche admits obliquely that she knows about sexual desire ('when the devil is in you') but it seems that she has never experienced true passion in which love and sexual desire play equal parts. It may be that she is too absorbed in herself ever to surrender herself.

Blanche may hide her alcoholism behind her euphemisms but she does recognise some of her weaknesses ('I've got to be good and keep my hands off children' – Scene 5). The weakness that she never does admit, and may not be aware of, is the reckless streak in her, which makes her risk her chance of security in the episode with the young man in Scene 5 and, repeatedly, when entertaining Mitch in Scene 6.

Significantly she never speaks of this except when telling herself to be good: her actions on the stage alone speak here. Perhaps this is because she herself is uncertain about her motives for such behaviour. The readers too can only speculate, and it is arguable that the uncertainty about some aspects of Blanche's character may well contribute to making her a believable human being.

Tennessee Williams himself apparently came to see her as a real woman who went on living outside his play. He remarked later that Blanche was a real survivor and that he was sure that she would recover and leave the asylum and marry a 'Gentleman Caller' (Tennessee Williams's title of a film script, later his play *The Glass Menagerie*).

STANLEY

A similar method of characterisation was used by Tennessee Williams when building up the character of Stanley Kowalski. The stage directions introducing him in Scene 1 give his physical description, stressing his animal sexuality, his machismo. He is meant to be seen as the cock of the walk, '*the gaudy seed-bearer*' in the playwright's striking phrase. His basic contempt for women may be gathered from the way he addresses the sisters during the poker game in Scene 3 ('You hens cut out that conversation in there!'). He abuses his friends as well, but they respond with loyalty and even affection.

Stanley's ungrammatical speech betrays his lack of education, but he is shrewd, sensing quite early in his acquaintance with Blanche that some aspects of her behaviour are out of keeping with what is expected of a Southern lady. Her drinking is no secret to him either, as Mitch tells Blanche in Scene 9.

He is quite as class-conscious as Blanche herself. Having married a gentlewoman, he is acutely aware and resentful of the differences in outlook and manner between himself and his wife. It is therefore inevitable that there should be hostility between him and Blanche, who is trying to make Stella revert to the past of Belle Reve.

It is equally inevitable, given Stanley's awareness of his masculinity and his contempt for women, that the hostility should be expressed through sexual domination.

The way the play has been constructed, with the rape as the climax in the penultimate scene, and the last scene centred on Blanche's departure, leaves some questions unanswered. Was there a confrontation between Stanley and Blanche in which he denied her accusation? What went on during those weeks between the rape and Blanche's departure?

Such questions in the readers' minds refer of course only to the action of the play, but they have a bearing on Stanley's character as well as on that of his wife. His machismo and his need to dominate are two aspects of his character that are stressed throughout the play in order to make the rape plausible. Could it be said that here Tennessee Williams sacrificed subtlety of character to the demands of the plot?

STELLA

There is a degree of ambiguity about Stella's character. The stage directions in Scene 1 offer little information beyond '*a gentle young woman ... of a background obviously quite different from her husband's*'. The readers learn about her from the other characters' comments, especially Blanche's, when she remarks on her sister's quiet, reserved manner. Gradually the readers may grow aware of a dry irony in Stella's brief remarks which implies an independence of mind and a certain hardness.

What strikes us most about Stella is her passionate love for her husband. Strong sexuality is something the sisters share. Blanche is led by it into promiscuity which will eventually take her into the mental hospital. For Stella it is channelled into an overpowering passion for her husband which will make Blanche's committal unavoidable.

Stella's surrender to Stanley is almost total: she has accepted his world and its values. We need to be convinced of her devotion to her husband if we are to accept as believable her complicity in Blanche's committal. Given that Stella cannot imagine life without Stanley, her readiness to sacrifice her sister becomes inevitable. She will carry her guilt (as Tennessee Williams accepted his imagined share of responsibility for his sister's lobotomisation and subsequent committal) as a price to be paid for the preservation of her marriage.

Characters may take on a life of their own beyond the confines of a play, as we have seen in Tennessee Williams's comment on Blanche. When it comes to Stella and Stanley we might be permitted to wonder if the comic characters of Eunice and Steve were not introduced to foreshadow the Kowalskis' later years – Stella slovenly, fat and blowzy after too many pregnancies, and Stanley, no longer the '*gaudy seed-bearer*', but a fat, wheezing patron of the local prostitutes.

MITCH

In the interplay of characters in *A Streetcar Named Desire* Mitch too has a part. Shy, clumsy, slow-thinking, he is a foil to the shrewd, loud, domineering Stanley, and of course also to the poetry-loving, fanciful Blanche. When in Scene 9 he tears Blanche's paper lantern off the light bulb, the harshness of his action shocks like a rape, and ironically his own half-hearted attempt at raping Blanche fails, and the act is carried out by his hero Stanley the same night.

The depiction of Mitch's character depends entirely on the dialogue, on other people's comments on him, and on his own self-deprecating remarks about himself. His role is to offer Blanche the promise of a safe haven, to spur Stanley indirectly to find out about Blanche's past in order to protect his old buddy. Also, as Tennessee Williams hints in Scene 3, Mitch's interest in Blanche encourages Stanley to think of her as sexually desirable, and is yet another factor in the catastrophic climax of Scene 10.

Throughout the play the emphasis is on the characters' natures which make them act in the way they do. The inevitability of fate that is at the heart of drama is created by the characters being what they are, by acting as they do because their natures compel them. The author's skill lies in taking the human qualities necessary for the enactment of the tragedy, and building from them, through speech and action, believable human beings.

THEMES

DESIRE AND FATE

The theme that dominates the play is contained in its arresting and memorable title. There really was a streetcar in New Orleans that carried the word 'Desire' as its destination, and another that went to 'Cemeteries'. When Tennessee Williams was living in New Orleans in 1946, and was working on *A Streetcar Named Desire* he was so struck by the names of these two streetcars that he mentioned them in an essay he wrote at the time: 'Their indiscourageable progress up and down Royal Street struck me as having some symbolic bearing of a broad nature on the life in the Vieux Carré – and everywhere else for that matter' (quoted in *The Kindness of Strangers: The Life of Tennessee Williams* by Donald Spoto, p. 129).

A streetcar running unswervingly along the rails to its destination could be seen as a symbol of the inexorability of fate. To Tennessee Williams, however, the streetcar's destination, 'Desire', spoke of more than an undefined force of fate. The force that drives Blanche to her destruction is desire, sexual passion. In Scene 4 when the sisters speak of sexual desire, Blanche uses the same image of a streetcar for it, 'that rattle-trap street-car', and Stella ripostes, 'Haven't you ever ridden on that street-car?' They both know what they are talking about – and so did the playwright himself.

Throughout his life Tennessee Williams was driven from one sexual encounter to another, exactly like Blanche, and like Blanche he too seemed incapable of committing himself to a permanent relationship, in his case homosexual. When Blanche longs for Mitch to marry her, she is not seeking a permanent sexual relationship but the material security of a home of her own ('The poor man's Paradise – is a little peace' – Scene 9).

To be driven by desire, Tennessee Williams seems to be saying, is self-destructive, yet the victims of an overpowering passion are carried along helplessly, unable to escape. Blanche's fate is foreordained, and the playwright stresses this in the streetcar image. We might say that Stella too is driven by the same force, having abandoned herself to her passionate love for Stanley. What her final destination might be is not shown – except perhaps in Eunice?

There is another image of fate in the play, one with a very respectable literary lineage. In Scenes 4, 6 and 10 Tennessee Williams introduces a roaring locomotive at a dramatic moment (Blanche's condemnation of Stanley; her description of her husband's death; just before the rape), but the random introduction of the locomotive as a symbol of fate does not carry here the impact of the streetcar metaphor, though it had been used with considerable effect by other writers (Leo Tolstoy in *Anna Karenina*, 1875–7, Emile Zola in *La Bête Humaine*, 1890).

It may be that Tennessee Williams had originally intended the locomotive as the **leitmotiv** of his play, but was so struck by the irony of a lurching streetcar with the grand name 'Desire' that he abandoned his original plan.

DEATH

The streetcar to 'Desire' was linked in Tennessee Williams's mind with another going to 'Cemeteries'. This fortuitous reminder of the likely eventual outcome of a life driven by passion served to reinforce the theme of fatal desire.

Images of death recur throughout the play. Blanche's descriptions of the deaths at Belle Reve, though oblique, contain enough gruesome detail to make their impact felt – the dying woman so swollen by disease that her body could not be fitted into a coffin, but had to be 'burned like rubbish' (Scene 1); the 'blood-stained pillow-slips' which Blanche had to change because there were no longer any servants to do it (Scene 9). Blanche's dream of being 'buried at sea sewn up in a clean white sack' (Scene 11) is equally chilling, perhaps because of her emphasis on a clean sack.

One significant death that cannot be forgotten throughout the play, is the suicide of Blanche's young husband. Its own polka music reminds us insistently of the tragedy. It recurs, the music in Blanche's mind growing louder until it stops with the fatal shot. The shock of the discovery of her husband's homosexuality and her guilt at his subsequent suicide after she had blurted out her disgust, partly account for her mental instability, her promiscuity and her alcoholism, the three contributory factors in her tragedy.

Tennessee Williams himself was obsessed with death, perhaps because of a nearly fatal illness in childhood. In later years his terror of disease, especially of cancer, and of dying took the form of a dangerous obsessive hypochondria. The reminders of death throughout the play, which echo his own private terrors, culminate in the symbolic figure of the Mexican seller of flowers for the dead (Scene 9). This figure plays a similar part to the grotesque shadows surrounding Blanche in Scene 10. The realism of the earlier scenes is abandoned in order to give these symbolic figures the prominence that Tennessee Williams gave them in his own mind.

MADNESS

Blanche's fear of madness is first hinted at in Scene 1 ('I *can't* be *alone*! Because – as you must have noticed – I'm – *not* very *well* …'). Never stable even as a girl, she was shattered by her husband's suicide and the circumstances surrounding it. Later the harrowing deaths at Belle Reve with which she evidently had to cope on her own, also took their toll. By this time she had begun her descent into promiscuity and alcoholism, and in order to blot out the ugliness of her life she created her fantasy world of adoring respectful admirers, of romantic songs and gay parties.

She is never entirely successful at this, as the memories of her husband's suicide remain persistently alive in her mind, always accompanied by the polka music. Drink is her solace on these occasions as she waits for the sound of the shot that signals the end of the nightmare. It seems that she has learned to live with this, as she remarks to Mitch in a matter-of-fact way, 'There now, the shot! It always stops after that!' (Scene 9).

She has reached an accommodation with the nightmares in her mind, but she cannot bear the intrusion of ugly reality into her make-believe world. Stanley's revelations of her past, Mitch's rejection of her as 'not clean enough' and his clumsy attempt at raping her, and finally her rape by Stanley on the night when her sister is giving birth to his child – all these break her and her mind gives way. She retreats into her make-believe world, making her committal to an institution inevitable.

Like the other major themes of the play – desire and fate, and death – madness too was Tennessee Williams's obsession. His sister Rose's strange behaviour which had long been a source of anxiety to her parents, later took the form of violent sexual fantasies and accusations against her father. Her parents had her committed to an institution. Following the medical practice of the time a pre-frontal lobotomy was carried out, and Rose calmed down, certainly, but was left with no memories, no mind. Not only did Tennessee Williams feel guilty for not having saved Rose from all this, but he now feared for his own sanity because the mental illness that afflicted Rose might be hereditary. He certainly did have a breakdown of sorts in his early twenties.

All three major themes of *A Streetcar Named Desire* reflected his own private terrors which gave the edge to his writing. He brought empathy to the character of Blanche and the circumstances of her collapse.

DRAMATIC TECHNIQUES

THE UNITIES

The convention of imposing rules on playwrights is a long-held tradition. The so-called three **unities** – of time (demanding that the action of a play should take place within twenty-four hours), of place (requiring the setting to remain the same throughout the play) and of action (never so clearly defined as the other two unities, this was an insistence that the play should centre on the main characters, with no sub-plots, and that the action should have a satisfying ending) – were wrongly attributed by Renaissance literary critics to Aristotle, the Greek philosopher and critic. Whilst Aristotle certainly discussed several Greek tragedies, he never laid down any strict rules.

Nevertheless, from the fifteenth century onwards the three unities were discussed by critics, and observed – or broken (notably by Shakespeare) – by dramatists. Though not strictly adhered to, these rules still provided a framework within which a playwright could build a play.

During his years at the University of Missouri and at Washington University, Tennessee Williams read avidly, especially the modern European dramatists – August Strindberg, Henrik Ibsen and Anton Chekhov – all of whom wrote plays centred on a single character, which of course ensured the unity of action. (The other two unities had over the centuries lost their significance.)

If we look at *A Streetcar Named Desire*, the first thing to strike us is the unity of place, the entire action taking place in the Kowalskis' apartment or outside it. The action stretches over several months, starting in May, reaching its climax in September, with the tragic aftermath happening some weeks later. In other words, like many other playwrights, Tennessee Williams disregards the artificiality of the unity of time and instinctively adopts the unities of place and action.

STRUCTURE

Distinct from the theoretical rules of the **unities** there are certain practical considerations to which dramatists must pay attention.

Amongst these is the attention span of the audience. Trivial as this sounds, it is a serious consideration if the dramatist is to hold his audience. There have been exceptionally long plays, such as Shakespeare's *Henry IV, Parts I and II* (1597), if the two parts are performed together, or Eugene O'Neill's *Long Day's Journey into Night* (1956), but very long plays are rare.

As a concession to both the attention span of the audience and the physical stamina of the cast, the convention developed of dividing plays into Acts.

In Elizabethan tragedy there were no stage sets, the author's words providing a verbal picture of the background. Changes of setting were therefore easy. With the arrival of painted scenery and realistic props in the eighteenth and nineteenth centuries changes of setting became technically quite difficult and also costly. Authors were now expected to limit settings to a few, each change of scenery dictating the length of an Act.

Of course nowadays advanced lighting techniques and a revolving stage offer the possibility of doing away with the conventional division into Acts, yet the convention persists to a large extent.

Tennessee Williams, however, divides *A Streetcar Named Desire* into eleven scenes, with no break for an interval indicated. Inevitably there have been speculations on his reasons for this. One reason suggested is that Tennessee Williams was particularly successful in writing short one-act plays, and that he may have found it difficult to sustain dramatic tension for the length of a conventional Act. In this context we might note that *The Glass Menagerie* (1944) is divided into seven scenes, and *Camino Real* (1953) into sixteen 'blocks'.

Certainly if we examine the eleven scenes in *A Streetcar Named Desire* we find that each of them leads naturally to a climax, either a dramatic gesture (in Scene 1 Blanche sinks back, her head in her arms, to be sick) or a punchline (Blanche again, in Scene 3, 'I need kindness now', or in Scene 6, 'Sometimes – there's God – so quickly!'). The effect is of the closing scene of a playlet with the players motionless in a *tableau vivant*.

Another possible reason may be that Tennessee Williams who grew up in the Thirties, the golden age of Hollywood cinema, absorbed certain film techniques. We should remember here that he was the film critic for his high school magazine, paying close attention to the films he was reviewing.

His sequence of scenes (within which the action always moves quite quickly) might be compared to the camera witnessing one incident and moving on to another, taking in a whole scene or focusing on one face. The adaptability of Tennessee Williams's plays for the screen was certainly not lost on Hollywood, nor was his bold use of sensational scenes of violence and sexual passion, so dear to the film moguls. Fifteen of his plays were made into films, with Tennessee Williams collaborating on the scripts for seven of them.

VISUAL AND SOUND EFFECTS

The visual aspect of *A Streetcar Named Desire* was clearly very important to the author, partly perhaps as a result of his interest in the cinema. His stage directions are very detailed, aiming to create an atmosphere that would heighten the impact of the action. Even a cursory glance at the stage effects demanded in Scenes 9 and 10, for instance, will show the importance of this. In Scene 9 the Mexican flower-seller is a portent of death, while in Scene 10 grotesque menacing shapes, jungle noises and distorted music are employed to reflect Blanche's terror. That the visual side of a stage presentation mattered greatly to Tennessee Williams may be noticed particularly in Scene 3 where a Van Gogh painting is evoked in the stage directions.

As well as visual effects sound effects are also used. Foremost among them are the 'blue piano' representing the spirit of the rundown quarter, the polka for Blanche's guilty memories of her husband, harsh discords for the rape and for Blanche's removal to the mental hospital.

Perhaps the use of music is again a technique learnt from the cinema? Tennessee Williams uses it effectively, though the readers of the play naturally have to employ their imagination here – as the director of a play does in the early stages of work. In a sense the readers will be staging their own performance of the play in their minds. Naturally it can never be a complete performance with all the details in place, but perhaps it will make up in nuances of mood for what it lacks in definition.

FOCUS

Though far from being the heroine of classical tragedy, Blanche still commands our attention. She appears in every scene, and if you glance at the eleven scenes (see Dramatic Technique on Structure) you will notice that the final tableau of each scene more often than not centres on her, and that she speaks the punchline.

In the last scene particularly this pathetic deluded woman acquires the dignity she has been lacking. Her irritating mannerisms fall away, and she leaves on the doctor's arm with the famous line 'Whoever you are – I have always depended on the kindness of strangers'.

She leaves, ignorant of what lies ahead of her, and the pathos of her ignorance has the effect of somehow diminishing those whom she is leaving without a backward glance: the hysterical Stella, the blustering bully Stanley. In a pointed contrast to Scene 3 this time the poker players stand up awkwardly as she passes through. The echo of the earlier scene is stressed by the repetition of Blanche's words. It draws our attention to the changed circumstances and to the change in Blanche herself.

The **hubris** of Greek tragedy – the humiliation of an arrogant person – is curiously reversed here, as the vain, self-deluded Blanche acquires tragic stature after her downfall. Having been at the centre of the play throughout, Blanche stages a dramatic exit. Stanley's lovemaking to Stella provides an ironic **coda**: she had bartered her sister for sexual gratification, and the bargain is now completed.

HANDLING OF TIME

The action of the play covers a period of some five months. The first six scenes stretch over the first few days of Blanche's visit in May, but Scene 7 moves abruptly to mid September when Scenes 7 to 10 take place within one day. The last scene follows a few weeks later.

In other words there is a cluster of dramatic events in May and another in September, by which time some relationships have crystallised (Stanley's dislike of Blanche as an intruder and a potential rival with both Stella and Mitch; Mitch's hesitant courtship of Blanche), and some of the obscure references to the past have become clear (the loss of Belle Reve; the suicide of Blanche's husband and the reasons for it; the reason for Blanche's departure from Laurel; her hopeless material and emotional situation).

The first group of scenes sets the stage for the calamities that will take place in the second group, and the last scene, which takes place some weeks later, shows the outcome of these events. We have touched on the possible reasons for Tennessee Williams's choice of eleven short scenes instead of the conventional three to five Acts (see Dramatic Technique on Structure). It might also be useful to consider here the grouping of the scenes into two clusters, with the last scene set apart both in mood and in tension.

Though Scenes 1–6 set the stage for the second cluster of scenes, their function cannot be said to be purely preparatory. Dramatic incidents, violence and passion figure in all of them, in varying degrees. It may be said that there is a sense of restraint in the first group (except for the drunken incident in Scene 3 which can be accepted as part of the pattern for Stanley's poker nights), of waiting for what the future will bring. The anticipation of disaster is muted, though the readers (or audience) already accept that there will be no happy ending.

In the second group Tennessee Williams makes it quite clear that, as Blanche says in Scene 10, 'Some awful thing will happen'. In Scene 7 there is Stanley's denunciation of Blanche and her contrapuntal singing off-stage, blissfully ignorant of what is being said. In Scene 8 the mounting tension culminates in Stanley's cruel birthday present of a bus ticket back to Laurel. In Scene 9 the first of the symbolic – one might say **Expressionist** – figures appears, the Mexican seller of flowers for the dead, followed by Mitch's attempt at raping Blanche. The readers or audience may have guessed what will follow in the next scene. Scene 10 starts amiably enough, with Stanley even offering to 'bury the hatchet', but soon the tone of the conversation, and the mood of the set, changes. As Stanley strips off Blanche's pretensions, menacing shapes appear on the walls of the apartment and the street outside is filled with violence. The climax is now inevitable, foreshadowed by Blanche's terror.

The difference between the two groups of scenes, then, lies in the degree of hostility and violence. The first group could be seen as Act I, establishing the characters and the relationships between them, while the second group might be regarded as a violent second Act, with Scene 11 as a short last Act, closing the play.

Time is used as a dramatic device, the scenes following one another first slowly, then at speed, creating the tension inherent in a violent, tragic end that is inescapable.

One more aspect of Tennessee Williams's treatment of time must be mentioned: the significant features of the plot, in particular Blanche's promiscuity and her drinking, and her part in the loss of Belle Reve, are given not chronologically, but through oblique references throughout the play (see Textual Analysis: Text 1 for references to this).

Two levels of language are used in *A Streetcar Named Desire* – the words spoken by the characters in the play and the text of the stage directions. Whether witnessing a performance or reading the text of a play we rely on the dialogue to enable us to create an image of the characters, to decide if we like or dislike them, to try to understand them and their actions. The nuances of speech set the characters in their class context and show the differences of social status and education as well as of character. In *A Streetcar Named Desire* the very marked differences between Stanley and Blanche are stressed by Stanley's non-grammatical, coarse, often slangy speech as against Blanche's high-flown rhetoric which often rings false (as it is meant to), and never lets us forget that she was a teacher of English. At times there is a lyrical quality in her words, emphasising their emotional content.

Stella too speaks correct English, but in a matter-of-fact, mostly unemotional tone, except when she speaks of her love for her husband.

Eunice and Steve are set firmly a rung or two below Stanley on the class ladder, again by their use of language as much as by their drunken public quarrels.

Mitch too is defined by the way he speaks: his efforts at speaking properly are marred by grammatical slip-ups as much as by his genteel circumlocutions ('I perspire', never 'I sweat'). He cannot follow or match Blanche's flights of fancy, and is acutely aware of this.

As we have seen, the language of the characters in a play is the most important way of defining their nature, their social status and their emotional make-up. Try to imagine forming an idea of the people in this play from their actions alone. The result would be flat, often incomprehensible unless the actors adopted the exaggerated gestures of mime.

Only their speech gives them life, and it is a measure of the dramatist's art that he can turn characters into credible human beings by what they say and how they say it. The words he chooses to put into their mouths and the way he makes them speak are all-important.

Another kind of diction can of course be found in a play – in the stage directions. As we have seen, Tennessee Williams's stage directions are unusually detailed, ensuring that the sets evoke the right atmosphere. However, they are also remarkable for another reason – they are beautifully written, evocative, accurate, and employ poetic images to convey their meaning. In this respect they are quite unusual.

In *A Dictionary of Literary Terms* by Martin Gray (Longman, 1984) **imagery** is defined as 'the figurative language in a piece of literature', that is, words referring to objects or qualities, which have the power to appeal to the senses and emotions of the reader. **Metaphors** and **similes** are the typical stock-in-trade of **figurative language**, though of course there are many other figures of speech (**tropes**) also employed.

Symbolism on the other hand is the use of something to represent a quality or a concept on the basis of some similarity between the symbol and the thing it represents. For instance, a peacock may represent vanity, or a lion strength. These two examples may be described as conventional symbols, readily understood by everyone.

Writers often use symbols that are not so easily understood because they are based on private experiences, on a personal vision of the world and life. Precisely because such symbols are not readily understood, and require either some knowledge of the writer's life or an instinctive empathy with the thinking behind the symbol, they are much more challenging and intriguing to the reader.

In *A Streetcar Named Desire* the imagery of the stage directions will attract the readers' attention. It is to be expected that Tennessee Williams should make use of the evocative power of figurative language when he is trying to paint a word picture or convey in words the quality of a sound. Thus in Scene 1 the phrase '*the infatuated fluency of brown fingers*' conveys the black pianist's skilful playing, his total absorption in the music, and his pleasure in it.

In Scene 11 the 'Varsouviana' polka is '*filtered into weird distortion*' in Blanche's mind, the harsh discords signalling that the sad memories of the past are about to give way to a cruel institutionalised future.

The use of imagery is however not limited to Tennessee Williams's stage directions alone. When Blanche is moved, she frequently uses figurative language, as befits a teacher of English. So for instance we find in Scene 5 'Have got to be seductive – put on soft colours, the colours of butterfly wings, and glow'; in Scene 6 she describes love as being like 'a blinding light on something that had always been half in shadow'; and in Scene 10 she speaks of the paddy-wagon picking up drunken soldiers 'like daisies'.

While from Blanche such figurative language is to be expected, surprisingly we find Stanley too using metaphors when he is moved. His phrase the 'coloured lights' used twice in Scene 8 to describe the ecstasy of passion is startling and evocative, as is his contemptuous description of Blanche's evening gown and tiara as 'that worn-out Mardi Gras outfit, rented for fifty cents from some rag-picker' (Scene 10).

When it comes to **symbolism**, the first symbol to strike the reader is of course the streetcar bound for Desire or Cemeteries, which represents not only Blanche's headlong descent into disaster, but Tennessee Williams's lifelong pursuit of sexual partners. (See Themes for discussion of this and other symbols. It is to be expected that a writer like Tennessee Williams should express his private terrors in symbols.) The streetcar is also used by both sisters as a euphemism for sexual experience in Scene 4. The headlong rush of a locomotive is another symbol of relentless fate (Scenes 4, 6 and 10).

Like the streetcar to Desire, the one going to Elysian Fields is an obvious symbol, used ironically, as the Elysian Fields – the abode of the blessed dead in Greek mythology – turn out to be a rundown street in New Orleans.

The spilt coke on Blanche's skirt is another symbol, recalling the blood spilt by her husband's suicide. Of course, her endless baths are an obvious symbol of her unspoken desire to be cleansed of her guilt for her husband's death and of her promiscuous past. Ritual cleansing has a long history, going back to Pontius Pilate who 'took water and washed his hands' after the Jews had demanded the death of Jesus (Matthew 26:24).

Again her Chinese paper lantern hiding the naked light bulb is a symbol of Blanche's longing for what she calls magic (Scene 9), the dressing up of ugly reality. It is linked also with the image of a moth fatally attracted by light.

It is noticeable that these symbols centre round Blanche. This is understandable – after all she is the focus of this play, the character with whom Tennessee Williams identified most, and, moreover, one whose great need was to find another reality in her imagination.

The use of distorted shapes and jungle cries as symbols of human cruelty (Scenes 10 and 11) are further examples of such effective techniques.

As well as symbols expressed in words or by visual effects Tennessee Williams rather unusually uses music for the purpose of driving home a message. The 'blue piano' is a symbol of the callous vitality of the Vieux

Carré of New Orleans, while the 'Varsouviana' polka represents the tragedy in Blanche's past.

The significance of both musical themes goes beyond merely providing a touch of local colour – they mark a change of atmosphere, convey a menace, underline a tragic development. The 'blue piano' in particular can signal a variety of messages whereas the polka is specifically linked with the suicide of Blanche's husband and is heard by her only when she remembers him. Both symbols will of course be appreciated more keenly by the theatre audience, with the printed stage directions offering only a poor substitute to the readers of the play.

On another level Stanley and Blanche are the symbols of two Americas: the new America of the immigrants, urban, egalitarian, ruthless, vibrantly alive, against the decadent old plantation culture rooted in the slavery system.

All these symbols are used deliberately. A dramatist will naturally think in images to express the emotions that inspired his or her play. It is the readers' (or spectators') exciting task to identify the symbols and try to interpret them. Most of Tennessee Williams's symbols are easy to read – and are no less effective dramatically for that. Of course, the readers of the play have the time to look for other symbols, less obvious perhaps – for example Blanche's drinking as a way to oblivion; her fragility like that of a moth.

PART FOUR

TEXTUAL ANALYSIS

In the Detailed Summaries, Tennessee Williams's play was analysed scene by scene, starting with a summing up of the action, followed by a comment on the author's handling of the scene, and concluding with explanatory notes on the words and phrases used in the scene.

Here by contrast we concentrate on three short extracts from the play, each one just a page or so in length. The analysis will be more detailed, giving due weight to the words and phrases which might not attract special attention in the summary of a whole scene.

In the course of the analysis we should gain insights beyond our appreciation of the verbal skills of the dramatist. The words he uses are, after all, the sole tool of his trade. The actors' speeches, admittedly in Tennessee Williams's case greatly aided by the stage directions, have to convey the dramatic developments (tell the story, so to speak) and also indirectly to build up the characters whom the actors represent on the stage, and establish the background of the action.

It is clear, then, that the words spoken on the stage (or read in a printed version of the play) are quite uniquely important. As in a poem, each word is chosen with great care, and should be spoken or read with equal care.

TEXT 1   (SCENE 1, PAGES 12–13)

STELLA: Stop this hysterical outburst and tell me what's happened? What do you mean fought and bled? What kind of –

BLANCHE: I knew you would, Stella. I knew you would take this attitude about it!

STELLA: About – what? – please!

BLANCHE [*slowly*]: The loss – the loss ...

STELLA: Belle Reve? Lost, is it? No!

BLANCHE: Yes, Stella.

They stare at each other across the yellow-checked linoleum of the table. BLANCHE *slowly nods her head and* STELLA *looks slowly down at her hands folded on the table. The music of the "blue piano" grows louder.* BLANCHE *touches her handkerchief to her forehead.*

STELLA: But how did it go? What happened?

BLANCHE [*springing up*]: You're a fine one to ask me how it went!

STELLA: Blanche!

BLANCHE: You're a fine one to sit there *accusing me* of it!

STELLA: *Blanche!*

BLANCHE: I, I, *I* took the blows in my face and my body! All of those deaths! The long parade to the graveyard! Father, mother! Margaret, that dreadful way! So big with it, it couldn't be put in a coffin! But had to be burned like rubbish! You just came home in time for the funerals, Stella. And funerals are pretty compared to deaths. Funerals are quiet, but deaths – not always. Sometimes their breathing is hoarse, and sometimes it rattles, and sometimes they even cry out to you, "Don't let me go!" Even the old, sometimes, say, "Don't let me go." As if you were able to stop them! But funerals are quiet, with pretty flowers. And, oh, what gorgeous boxes they pack them away in! Unless you were there at the bed when they cried out, "Hold me!" you'd never suspect there was the struggle for breath and bleeding. You didn't dream, but I saw! *Saw! Saw!* And now you sit there telling me with your eyes that I let the place go! How in hell do you think all that sickness and dying was paid for? Death is expensive, Miss Stella! And old Cousin Jessie's right after Margaret's, hers! Why, the Grim Reaper had put up his tent on our doorstep! ... Stella. Belle Reve was his headquarters! Honey – that's how it slipped through my fingers! Which of them left us a fortune? Which of them left a cent of insurance even? Only poor Jessie – one hundred to pay for her coffin. That was all, Stella! And I with my pitiful salary at the school. Yes, accuse me! Sit there and stare at me, thinking I let the place go! *I* let the place go? Where were *you*. In bed with your – Polack!

STELLA [*springing*]: Blanche! You be still! That's enough! [*She starts out.*]

BLANCHE: Where are you going?

STELLA: I'm going into the bathroom to wash my face.

BLANCHE: Oh, Stella, Stella, you're crying!

STELLA: Does that surprise you?

The first of the three passages, taken from the introductory scene of the play, demonstrates Tennessee Williams's skill in writing dialogue that adds to our understanding of the characters, and also to our store of information about earlier events that have built up the dramatic tensions of the play.

The passage begins during a heated exchange between Stella and Blanche. The two sisters have met, embraced and spoken lightly (and in Blanche's case a trifle condescendingly) about New Orleans, about the Kowalskis' humble apartment, and about Stella's husband. A point has been made about Blanche's nervous state.

Blanche appears ill at ease, and finds it difficult to reveal what she clearly feels she must reveal – the loss of the family mansion, Belle Reve. She expects to be blamed by her sister, and the readers (or spectators) may sense that she does feel guilty and is forestalling any reproaches by her accusations of Stella.

Stella tries to extract the plain facts of the matter from her sister, but Blanche refuses to cooperate. In a long speech, full of unspoken (but strongly hinted at) horrors of her life at Belle Reve she speaks of her own suffering and of her sister's selfish indifference. The speech is accusatory and wounding, and is meant to be: we might remember here the saying that attack is the best defence. The scene ends with Stella in tears, going off to wash her face.

The passage is just one page long, yet we learn a great deal from it. First, the two sisters are quite unlike one another in emotional make-up. Stella interrupts her sister's self-dramatising reproaches with a cutting comment on Blanche's 'hysterical outburst' and on her emotionally loaded phrase 'fought and bled', which Stella repeats, probably ironically.

Blanche reacts at once by declaring that Stella's attitude was only to be expected. We are made aware that the confrontation follows a long-established pattern of rows between the sisters.

Blanche is slowly brought to admit that Belle Reve has been sold, and Stella's reaction to the shattering news is as typical of her as Blanche's histrionics are of Blanche. She 'looks slowly down at her hands folded on the table', her silence eloquent of her distress.

She wants to know the facts, though, and it becomes clear that this is something Blanche cannot, or will not, provide (her confrontation with Stanley in Scene 2 shows this quite clearly). This leaves it open to question whether her inability to give the details is due to her ignorance of business matters, or whether this is deliberate obfuscation of unpleasant and possibly damaging facts.

In Blanche's long speech we notice her use of a metaphor of physical injury ('I took the blows in my face and my body!') which echoes her earlier 'I fought and bled'.

The images of messy death, of blood and physical pain proliferate in her speech: Margaret so swollen with disease that she could not be fitted into a coffin and had to be burned like rubbish; the hoarse breathing, the death rattle of the dying, their desperate clinging to life ('Don't let me go!'), the bleeding (later, in Scene 9, Blanche tells Mitch of the 'blood-stained pillow-slips').

The readers grow aware that Blanche is now obsessed with death. She may speak jokingly of the 'Grim Reaper' who 'had put up his tent on our doorstep!', but the death scenes she had witnessed are stamped on her mind. Her experiences in her last years at Belle Reve clearly affected her already precarious mental balance. We may remember this later, in Scene 9, when the symbolic figure of the Mexican seller of paper flowers for the dead brings to Blanche's mind 'a house where dying old women remembered their dead men'.

Blanche's resentment of Stella's absence is obvious. She reminds her sister bitterly that she only came home for the funerals, which are quiet and 'pretty compared to deaths', with 'gorgeous' coffins and beautiful flowers. Some of her resentment is evidently due to sexual jealousy of her younger sister who got away, found a husband and was 'In bed with [her] Polack' while her sister watched over deathbeds.

Within this dramatic speech we (and Stella) find a few practical comments on the recurrent funeral expenses, not covered by insurance (except for Cousin Jessie's hundred dollars which just paid for her coffin, but not for her funeral). This sudden descent into practicalities is characteristic of Blanche: remember her in Scene 2 when, after her melodramatic outburst at Stanley's desecration of her dead husband's poems, she puts on her glasses to go methodically through a pile of legal documents concerning the mortgaging of Belle Reve.

In the last few lines of the passage we may notice Blanche's self-absorption, her inability to understand other people, as she appears surprised that her sister is crying (see Scene 6 in Detailed Summaries for this aspect of Blanche's character).

What do you mean fought and bled? the deliberate repetition is perhaps ironical, intended to lower the emotional temperature and so mock Blanche's histrionics

The loss – the loss Blanche still cannot bring herself to speak of the loss of the family mansion openly

the yellow-checked linoleum notice Tennessee Williams's attention to detail in the stage directions, and also his sensitivity to colour

touches her handkerchief to her forehead the theatrical gesture is typical of Blanche

accusing me of it! very revealing words: as Stella has not spoken a word of reproach, we can only assume that Blanche's own feelings of guilt are prompting her here. Later, in Scene 9, we learn that she already indulged in wild behaviour while still living at Belle Reve, and it may well be that her drinking and her one-night stands contributed to her inability to cope with the sorry financial state of Belle Reve, as much as the expensive funerals

The long parade to the graveyard! Blanche's obsession with death is rooted in her appalling experiences at Belle Reve. Her account is all the more affecting for what is left unsaid. We might also notice here the absence of any sentimentality, indeed of any emotional involvement, in her description of the deaths. Is this due to self-discipline, or is it again her self-absorption and lack of empathy?

my pitiful salary an appeal for sympathy, tinged maybe with self-dramatisation

in bed with your – Polack! a double insult: a hint at Stella's sexual appetite, and the contempt of a Southern aristocrat for a vulgar immigrant

That's enough! though she remained silent while Blanche was attacking her, Stella will not tolerate insults to her husband. We may remember here Stella's defence of Stanley in Scene 4

Stella, you're crying! Blanche seems surprised at this. Is it because Stella is usually firmly in control of herself, or is it that Blanche lacks the insight into other people's feelings, and so is surprised when her cutting words do inflict a wound?

TEXT 2   (SCENE 9, PAGE 72)

MITCH [*getting up*]: It's dark in here.

BLANCHE: I like it dark. The dark is comforting to me.

MITCH: I don't think I ever seen you in the light. [BLANCHE *laughs breathlessly.*] That's a fact!

BLANCHE: Is it?

MITCH: I've never seen you in the afternoon.

BLANCHE: Whose fault is that?

MITCH: You never want to go out in the afternoon.

BLANCHE: Why, Mitch, you're at the plant in the afternoon!

MITCH: Not Sunday afternoon. I've asked you to go out with me sometimes on Sundays but you always make an excuse. You never want to go out till after six and then it's always some place that's not lighted much.

BLANCHE: There is some obscure meaning in this but I fail to catch it.

MITCH: What it means is I've never had a real good look at you, Blanche.

BLANCHE: What are you leading up to?

MITCH: Let's turn the light on here.

BLANCHE [*fearfully*]: Light? Which light? What for?

MITCH: This one with the paper thing on it. [*He tears the paper lantern off the light bulb. She utters a frightened gasp.*]

BLANCHE: What did you do that for?

MITCH: So I can take a look at you good and plain!

BLANCHE: Of course you don't really mean to be insulting!

MITCH: No, just realistic.

BLANCHE: I don't want realism.

MITCH: Naw, I guess not.

BLANCHE: I'll tell you what I want. Magic! [MITCH *laughs.*] Yes, yes, magic! I try to give that to people. I misrepresent things to them. I don't tell truth, I tell what *ought* to be truth. And if that is sinful, then let me be damned for it! – *Don't turn the light on!*

MITCH *crosses to the switch. He turns the light on and stares at her. She cries out and covers her face. He turns the light off again.*

MITCH [*slowly and bitterly*]: I don't mind you being older than what I thought. But all the rest of it – God! That pitch about your ideals being so old-fashioned and all the malarkey that you've dished out all summer. Oh, I knew you weren't sixteen any more. But I was fool enough to believe you was straight.

The subject of this passage is the final confrontation between Mitch and Blanche. She, with the premonition of disaster (heralded by the polka music she alone hears), has been drinking, and is dishevelled and confused. Mitch is in his working clothes, unshaven, and slightly drunk. In their appearance they both show their distress.

To begin with, Blanche chatters incessantly, betraying her nervousness. Mitch's monosyllabic answers are in contrast to her high-flown, artificial speeches. Her flirtatiousness jars and adds to the dramatic tension. The readers (or spectators) expect an explosion of violence, which takes place in the part of the scene discussed here.

Mitch complains that the room is dark, and Blanche counters with her declaration that the dark is comforting to her. When Mitch tells her that he has never seen her in daylight, Blanche pretends not to understand him. In a shocking act of violence he then tears the Chinese paper lantern off the light bulb and turns the light on. Exposed to the harsh light Blanche cries out and covers her face while Mitch stares at her. The strong light has shown him her fading beauty, and in his eyes exposed also her pretence at virtue and innocence.

Emphasis on light and darkness here is striking, and we notice the reversal of conventional symbols. For Blanche light is a cruel enemy while darkness is kind. Mitch believes of course that this is simply because clear daylight will reveal that she is no longer young. This is true, but on a deeper, more important level for Blanche darkness hides the ugliness of the real world, enabling her to maintain her illusions. When her illusions go, so does her sanity.

She is remarkably clear-headed and frank about this. She declares 'I
don't tell truth, I tell what *ought* to be truth'. She presents herself as an
innocent girl to Mitch, because that is what he is looking for in her. More
importantly perhaps, that is how she wants to see herself, though she
repeatedly fails to maintain this illusion (as in her flirtation with the young
man in Scene 5, and in her crude invitation to Mitch in Scene 6, fortunately
spoken in French).

The fact that Mitch does not even remotely understand her
underlines the complete lack of empathy between them. Their relationship
is doomed to fail sooner or later. The way they speak again stresses the gulf
between them. Blanche's high-flown, artificial language (especially in the
conversation that immediately precedes the passage under discussion here)
is set against Mitch's short, contemptuous (and ungrammatical) replies.

Rhetoric against grunts, soft darkness against harsh light – the
message is that the relationship would have failed anyway.

The dark is comforting to me the dark hides Blanche's fading beauty and,
metaphorically, hides the ugliness of the cruel world around her

laughs breathlessly Blanche is nervous and frightened, and her laughter shows
it

There is some obscure meaning in this Blanche resorts once more to the stilted
educated speech of the schoolmistress in an attempt to regain control of the
situation

the paper lantern we now realise that Blanche's little purchase from the
Chinese shop in Scene 3 was intended by the author to play an even more
important role than occasioning her revealing remark to Mitch at the poker
party ('I can't stand a naked light bulb, any more than I can a rude remark or
a vulgar action'). Its real dramatic function is to be used in a metaphor for the
rape Mitch now has in mind. Stripping off the shade is a harsh, cruel action,
intended to hurt and humiliate

good and plain the words have perhaps a double meaning here: 'plain' can
mean 'ugly' as well as 'clear'. Blanche's response 'you don't really mean to be
insulting' shows that she is aware of the double meaning

I misrepresent things it is unusual for Blanche to be so frank. She is also quite
clear-headed about what she does and why. Earlier, in Scene 5, she admits to
Stella that she has had to pretend to be seductive, 'put a – paper lantern over
the light'. The words show that Blanche is aware of her need to camouflage

reality. On that earlier occasion she used metaphors throughout, evidently because she needed to disguise the truth. Now, knowing that she has lost Mitch, she is recklessly truthful ('then let me be damned for it!')

pitch Mitch's use of the word for a salesman's patter shows that Blanche's explanation of her motives is lost on him. To him she is simply deceitful, a liar pretending to be virtuous

TEXT 3   (SCENE 11, PAGES 84–85)

BLANCHE [*continuing*]: What's happened here? I want an explanation of what's happened here.

STELLA [*agonizingly*]: Hush! Hush!

EUNICE: Hush! Hush! Honey.

STELLA: Please, Blanche.

BLANCHE: Why are you looking at me like that? Is something wrong with me?

EUNICE: You look wonderful, Blanche. Don't she look wonderful?

STELLA: Yes.

EUNICE: I understand you are going on a trip.

STELLA: Yes, Blanche *is*. She's going on vacation.

EUNICE: I'm green with envy.

BLANCHE: Help me, help me get dressed!

STELLA [*handing her dress*]: Is this what you –

BLANCHE: Yes, it will do! I'm anxious to get out of here – this place is a trap!

EUNICE: What a pretty blue jacket.

STELLA: It's lilac coloured.

BLANCHE: You're both mistaken. It's Della Robbia blue. The blue of the robe in the old Madonna pictures. Are these grapes washed?

She fingers the bunch of grapes which EUNICE *has brought in.*

EUNICE: Huh?

BLANCHE: Washed, I said. Are they washed?

EUNICE: They're from the French Market.

BLANCHE: That doesn't mean they've been washed. [*The cathedral bells chime.*] Those cathedral bells – they're the only clean thing in the Quarter. Well, I'm going now. I'm ready to go.

EUNICE [*whispering*]: She's going to walk out before they get here.

STELLA: Wait, Blanche.

BLANCHE: I don't want to pass in front of those men.

EUNICE: Then wait'll the game breaks up.

STELLA: Sit down and …

BLANCHE *turns weakly, hesitantly about. She lets them push her into a chair.*

BLANCHE: I can smell the sea air. The rest of my time I'm going to spend on the sea. And when I die, I'm going to die on the sea. You know what I shall die of? [*She plucks a grape.*] I shall die of eating an unwashed grape one day out on the ocean. I will die – with my hand in the hand of some nice-looking ship's doctor, a very young one with a small blond moustache and a big silver watch. "Poor lady," they'll say, "the quinine did her no good. That unwashed grape has transported her soul to heaven." [*The cathedral chimes are heard.*] And I'll be buried at sea sewn up in a clean white sack and dropped overboard – at noon – in the blaze of summer – and into an ocean as blue as [*chimes again*] my first lover's eyes!

The last passage has an extraordinary dramatic force. On the surface it is a scene of domestic activity; Stella packing Blanche's trunk, Eunice gossiping, Blanche emerging from the bathroom. The group of poker players see through the portières in the kitchen, however, is ominously quiet, in deliberate contrast to their rowdiness in Scene 3.

The audience (and readers) are in ignorance of the meaning of the scene at first, like Blanche herself. There is complicity binding together Stella and Eunice, and the players, all of whom know what is going to happen.

Blanche, though ignorant of the situation, becomes aware of the tension and is frightened. Her 'Help me, help me get dressed!' is a thinly disguised plea for help as she feels she is caught in a trap. The other two women chatter on, flattering Blanche, complimenting her on her outfit.

This is very effective as a piece of theatre as the conventional small talk somehow emphasises the underlying tension.

The talk succeeds in distracting Blanche a little. Like a true schoolmistress she offers information about the correct name for the shade of blue of her jacket. She remains on edge, however, and her unease finds expression in her impatient, rather offhand remarks to Eunice ('Washed, I said ... That doesn't mean they've been washed').

Thinking of unwashed grapes starts her on an extraordinary flight of fancy of her death at sea, caused by eating an unwashed grape. She sees her own death in brilliantly clear colours, a pretty scene quite unlike what she had repeatedly witnessed at Belle Reve. The sketch of the young ship's doctor who will be by her side is strikingly detailed, idealised somewhat in the style of romantic fiction. He offers an ironic contrast to the real doctor from the mental hospital who will presently arrive to take her away. Perhaps this daydream of a pretty death with a handsome doctor beside her has prepared her to accept and trust the real doctor when he comes?

We notice also the emphasis on the purity of tone of the cathedral bells which are heard in the apartment for the first time now. The pure tone of the bell, the clean white sack in which she imagines herself buried at sea, both symbolise her longing for purification, for a cleansing from her sins, as did her frequent long baths. In the context, however, her dream of purity and of a peaceful death takes on an ironical meaning: the voyage she will undertake on the arm of the hospital doctor will take her to the harsh ugliness of a mental institution, an incarceration that will be a living death for her.

Her imaginary voyage set against the fast approaching reality gives the scene its painful tension. Throughout her speech she is answered by the unspoken thoughts of the others present in a dramatic counterpoint. This scene offers a splendid example of the dramatist's skill.

What's happened here? Blanche's agitated question shows that she senses that something momentous is happening

Is something wrong with me? Blanche is aware of the involuntary scrutiny by the other two women who know what is about to befall her

going on a trip ... going on vacation the euphemisms are cruelly ironical

The blue of the robe in the old Madonna pictures the image of the Virgin Mary is of course one of purity, of virginity

I don't want to pass in front of those men Blanche admits now that she is aware of the silent presence of the poker players, and fears them. The trauma she suffered at the hands of Mitch and especially Stanley, has made her afraid

an ocean as blue as ... my first lover's eyes the tone of romantic fiction is maintained

PART FIVE

Background

Tennessee Williams

Thomas Lanier Williams was born on 26 March 1911 in Columbus, Mississippi (the nickname 'Tennessee' was given to him later at college by a fellow student ignorant of the geography of the Southern states). His father, Cornelius Coffin Williams, was then an employee of a telephone company, and his mother Edwina, a typical spoilt, impractical Southern belle, was the daughter of a highly respected Episcopalian rector, the Rev. Walter E. Dakin.

There were three children born to the marriage, Thomas, or Tom, Rose, two years younger, and Dakin, born eight years after Tom. The Williams' marriage was not happy, and Mrs Williams turned more and more to the children and to the comfort of her parents' rectory. She enjoyed sharing her parents' position of esteem in a small town until her husband took up the post of manager in a shoe company in St Louis, and the family moved there in 1919.

The move was disastrous both for the children, who missed their grandparents' house, and for their mother who suddenly became a nonentity in a large city, losing her established status in Columbus. As the relations between husband and wife worsened Cornelius Williams started to drink heavily. At this time also Rose's behaviour began to cause concern. Tom suffered much from the unhappiness at home and found consolation in reading and later in writing.

In 1928 came a temporary respite when Tom was invited to accompany his grandfather, the Rev. Dakin, and a group of his parishioners on a trip to Europe. The liberating effect of this trip remained with Tom, and he returned to Europe regularly throughout his life.

In 1929 his grandparents' generosity enabled Tom to become a student at the University of Missouri, at Columbia. Not distinguished academically, he nevertheless profited greatly by his three years there. He read voraciously (in particular the modern European dramatists – Anton Chekhov, August Strindberg, Henrik Ibsen) and began to make a name for himself as a writer.

The Depression put an end to his studies, and in 1931 he became a clerk in the shoe firm employing his father. This was a miserable time for Tennessee Williams, and he suffered a breakdown. When his family's finances improved, he became a student at the Washington University in St Louis. He wrote a handful of plays, put on by small amateur companies.

An unhappy time followed, when his sister Rose became quite unstable mentally, and accused her father of attacking her. The sexual element in her fancies spelt scandal and so alarmed her mother that she agreed to a pre-frontal lobotomy to be performed on her daughter in 1937. Tennessee Williams was away at the State University of Texas at this time, and he never ceased to reproach himself for not having been there to prevent the operation. Nor could he ever forgive his mother for her part in the business. This harrowing time left its mark on Tennessee Williams, and on his work: *The Glass Menagerie* is obviously autobiographical, and there is much of Rose in the unstable Blanche of *A Streetcar Named Desire*.

There followed a period of drifting for Tennessee Williams which took him also to New Orleans. It seems that there he discovered his sexual identity and became a practising homosexual. Sexual liberation went hand in hand with confidence in his work. A collection of three short plays, *American Blues*, won a prize in 1939, and he was taken up by Audrey Wood, head of the best theatrical agency, the following year.

She obtained a contract with MGM for him as scriptwriter in 1943. Though his only script, *The Gentleman Caller*, was turned down by MGM, it became the basis of his first successful play, *The Glass Menagerie*. Moreover, scriptwriting certainly influenced the technique of his plays (see Dramatic Technique on Structure).

The successful staging of *A Glass Menagerie* in 1944 spurred Tennessee Williams on to his next major play, *A Streetcar Named Desire*. The writing of the play gave him some trouble, as witness the change of title (and of emphasis) from 'The Moth' to 'Blanche's Chair in the Moon' to 'The Poker Night' before finally, after his move to New Orleans, to *A Streetcar Named Desire*.

The play opened in 1947 and was a great success. Tennessee Williams was now a wealthy man, having sold the screen rights for both the plays, and deriving a good income from the stage productions as well.

The pattern of his life was now set for some time – visits to Europe, writing: a novel, *The Roman Spring of Mrs Stone* (1950); another film script, this time successful, *Baby Doll* (1951); several successful plays, *Camino Real* (1953), *Cat on a Hot Tin Roof* (1955), *Orpheus Descending* (1957), *Suddenly Last Summer* (1958), *Sweet Bird of Youth* (1959), *The Night of the Iguana* (1961).

Success did not seem to bring him happiness, though. He underwent psychotherapy for depression; his drug-taking and drinking grew worse, as did his frenetic search for sexual encounters, which caused much pain to his live-in partner for many years, Frank Merlo.

Tennessee Williams's writing deteriorated. Though he wrote several plays between 1962 and his death, none of them was really successful. By now he was so befuddled by drink and drugs (after an unsuccessful drastic treatment in a mental hospital to which he had been committed by his brother) that he seemed indifferent to his failures.

He died in New York on 24 February 1983 in a hotel named the Elysée (an ironically appropriate name that recalls the Elysian Fields in *A Streetcar Named Desire*). He choked to death on one of his barbiturates.

HIS OTHER WORKS

As is usually the case with writers who rely heavily on their own life story for inspiration, Tennessee Williams was always looking for subjects with which he could identify. It was a limitation but also the source of the strength and vividness of his writing. As he himself put it, 'Frankly there must be some limitations in me as a dramatist ... I must find characters who correspond to my own tensions' (quoted in *Tennessee Williams: Rebellious Puritan* by Nancy Tischler, p. 246).

Since his plays have a common source, that of his own life, they inevitably share several themes. The urge to look for pleasure, however destructive, which drove Tennessee Williams especially in his later years, is one. It is to be found in Blanche in *A Streetcar Named Desire* of course, and also in the homosexual Sebastian in *Suddenly Last Summer*, and in a female guise again in the ageing Princess Kosmonopolis in *Sweet Bird of Youth*.

The guilt Tennessee Williams felt about the institutionalisation of his sister Rose is paralleled by Stella's anguish at the close of *A Streetcar Named Desire*, and by Tom's remorse in *The Glass Menagerie*, the most directly autobiographical of all Tennessee Williams's plays.

Tennessee Williams's Southern-ness, his love of the South, not often openly declared, still imbues most of his work, either directly through the location and the leading characters, as in *Baby Doll*, *Cat on a Hot Tin Roof*, *Suddenly Last Summer*, or indirectly through nostalgic memories, based on what the Williams children heard often from their mother. *The Glass Menagerie* and *A Streetcar Named Desire* offer examples of such indirect inspiration.

In *The Glass Menagerie* Amanda's recollections of her youth evidently drew on Mrs Williams's nostalgic memories. The death of Bates Cutrere, one of Amanda's dashing beaux, is echoed by Blanche's traumatic experience of her husband's suicide. Even the location of both tragedies is the same, Moon Lake Casino.

Tennessee Williams's terror of dying of cancer is mirrored by Big Daddy's fears in *Cat on a Hot Tin Roof*. In *A Streetcar Named Desire*, however, for Blanche death comes like a bridegroom in her dream of dying at sea, though she had witnessed many sordid deaths at Belle Reve.

Finally a hidden theme that runs through *A Streetcar Named Desire* is the homosexuality of Blanche's husband which might be said to have shattered her life. In *Cat on a Hot Tin Roof* Maggie accuses her husband, Brick, of homosexuality, as does his father, Big Daddy, with disastrous consequences. In *Suddenly Last Summer* Sebastian is murdered and partly cannibalised by the native beggarboys on whom he had preyed. All the homosexual relationships in these plays end in disaster: was it Tennessee Williams's intention to placate morality? (See also Historical Background.)

One common characteristic of Tennessee Williams's plays is a sense of looming tragedy: the streetcar named Desire appears in other guises in all of Tennessee Williams's work.

Historical background

Although Tennessee Williams was working on *A Streetcar Named Desire* at the end of the Second World War, and the play was produced in 1947, only two years after the war, there is hardly any mention of the recent cataclysmic events in it (except for Stanley's brief reference to the Salerno landings in Scene 11). This characteristic omission is shared by all Tennessee Williams's plays.

The events that affected him, like most Southerners, were those of the American Civil War (1861–5). The Southern states tried – and failed – to secede from the Union in order to preserve their 'state rights', particularly the slavery system on which their flourishing tobacco and cotton industries were based. After their defeat the Southern states suffered a lengthy economic decline which contributed to the romantic appeal the South held for so many writers.

The Second World War and the cataclysmic political changes that followed, which included the rise of the United States to a world power, seemed to pass Tennessee Williams by. He seemed equally indifferent to a political issue that gained greatly in significance during his lifetime, and which might have been expected to have touched him closely: the question of gay rights. The politicising of what was basically a moral issue was successful in achieving its aims, and its impact on literature and the performing arts was great. Yet Tennessee Williams appeared unmoved by the movement or by its success.

The issue of homosexuality, so prominent in his private life, is certainly a strand in his work, but never the central theme, and certainly never taken up to be defended or pleaded for. We must remember of course that for the greater part of Tennessee Williams's life homosexuality was still illegal, though tolerated in some areas (New Orleans; Key West, Florida). This might explain his reluctance to give prominence to the issue.

According to Christopher Isherwood and others, however, there may have been another reason for Tennessee Williams's refusal to take up this cause. They believed that he hated being a homosexual, and could not accept those who came to terms with their sexual orientation (see *The Kindness of Strangers: The Life of Tennessee Williams* by Donald Spoto, p. 320).

When accused of never dealing with homosexuality openly, Tennessee Williams declared in an interview with *Gay Sunshine* that the main thrust of his work was not sexual orientation but social issues: 'I am not about to limit myself to writing about gay people' (quoted in *The Kindness of Strangers: The Life of Tennessee Williams* by Donald Spoto, p. 319).

Though he seemed to disapprove, yet he felt compelled to introduce homosexuality into his plays (Blanche might equally have found her husband in bed with a woman, though of course the dramatic effect would have been less shocking).

Not only was Tennessee Williams not interested in homosexuality as a political issue, but in several of his plays we sense his condemnation of it (*A Streetcar Named Desire*, *Cat on a Hot Tin Roof*, *Suddenly Last Summer*). A conflict existed then between his morality and his sexuality, never to be resolved, and never to be brought into the open in his plays, though the subject of gay rights was very much in the foreground of the political arena in the United States, especially during Tennessee Williams's later years.

LITERARY BACKGROUND

After the defeat of the Confederate army in 1865 the literature of the South revived and thrived on the nostalgia for the past, on regional rather than national patriotism and on the romantic appeal of a lost cause and a lost way of life. (A comparison might be made here with the romantic appeal of the Jacobite cause in Scottish writing, in works by such authors as Sir Walter Scott and Robert Louis Stevenson.)

The romanticising of the South went on into the twentieth century, and received a fresh impulse with the famous 1936 novel by Margaret Mitchell, *Gone with the Wind*, and especially with the phenomenal success of the 1939 film version of the novel.

Independent of this popular romantic image of the South, a new, specifically Southern literature emerged in the twentieth century. The fascination with the past merged gradually with an awareness of a South whose economic decay was symbolised by the decaying beauty of the planters' mansions (like Tennessee Williams's Belle Reve).

Greed and treachery were recognised as part of the Southern character in the novels of William Faulkner, set in the imaginary Yoknapatawpha county, of Thomas Wolfe, Erskine Caldwell, and Tennessee Williams's friend Carson McCullers.

One quality regarded as characteristic of the Southern writers was their rich imagination, often bordering on the bizarre and the grotesque ('Southern Gothic' was the phrase used to describe it). Its roots lay perhaps in an awareness of being part of a dying culture – dashing, romantic, and at the same time living on an economy based on deep injustice and cruelty. The cultural climate favoured the individualistic, the eccentric, the outcast.

This was the Southern culture that appealed to Tennessee Williams. His dislike of his mother had an adverse effect on his attitude to the romanticised South, but the South as a broken, damaged society with the ripe charms of decay, fired his imagination. As he himself said, 'I write out of love for the South … once a way of life that I am just old enough to remember – not a society based on money … I write about the South because I think the war between romanticism and the hostility to it is very sharp there' (quoted in *The Kindness of Strangers: The Life of Tennessee Williams* by Donald Spoto, p. 139).

The South seemed to him to stand for cultural values ignored by the money-grabbing, prosperous North (Blanche and Stanley may be seen as representing the two opposing sides).

The subject matter of his plays was deeply influenced by his image of the South, but he looked to the playwrights of Europe for models of the form. When a student at the University of Missouri, and already dreaming of a career as a playwright, Tennessee Williams immersed himself in the plays of Anton Chekhov, August Strindberg and Henrik Ibsen. August Strindberg's *Miss Julie* (1888) may well have influenced *A Streetcar Named Desire* in its equation of class antagonism with sexual tension.

Again, a parallel may be drawn between the plantation culture of Belle Reve and the household of Madame Ranevska in Anton Chekhov's *The Cherry Orchard* (1904). Both are doomed, useless, living extravagantly on the labour of others, yet they both possess a charm lacking equally in the blustering merchant Lopakhin in *The Cherry Orchard* and in Stanley Kowalski.

As for Henrik Ibsen, Tennessee Williams could have found no better model for constructing a play round one compelling central character than *Hedda Gabler* (1890), *The Master Builder* (1892), or *John Gabriel Borkman* (1896), to name a few among many.

The two cultures – the Southern and the European – meet successfully in *A Streetcar Named Desire*.

PART SIX

CRITICAL HISTORY

A Streetcar Named Desire was written and staged in the 1940s, a period when the American cinema was at the height of its popularity, and both theatre and cinema audiences were influenced by movies.

Tennessee Williams's play was a mixture of sex, violence and morality (present, however, only implicitly), a recipe tested out successfully in the cinema. The play drew also on the romantic myth of the American South, reinforced by the fantastic success of MGM's *Gone with the Wind* (1939).

Following the successful staging of *The Glass Menagerie* in 1944, *A Streetcar Named Desire* opened on 4 December 1947 to a very favourable reception by the critics of the *New York Daily News*, the *New York Post*, and the *New York Times* (which carried a glowing notice by Brooks Atkinson). The play won the Pulitzer Prize and the New York Drama Critics Circle Award. Interestingly there were also some less complimentary reviews (*Time* of 15 December 1947 declared that 'The play could stand more discipline ... there is sometimes an absence of form. And it could stand more variety: only the clash between Blanche and Stanley gets real emotion and drama into the play'. *Time* went on giving negative notices to Tennessee Williams's plays until 1962 when it suddenly called him 'the greatest living playwright anywhere').

In England *A Streetcar Named Desire* was by and large well received after its British première in 1949 (it was praised by, for instance, R.D. Smith in the *New Statesman* on 22 October 1949), though there were also some less favourable notices. Questions were asked in Parliament about the misuse of public funds in financing such an immoral play (this referred to an Arts Council grant towards the London production of the play).

Perhaps surprisingly, in view of the popular idea of French morality, when *A Streetcar Named Desire* opened in Paris in 1950, many disapproving voices were heard, and not just from the gallery: the reviews were rather less favourable than might have been expected.

A Streetcar Named Desire has been revived nine times since its first staging in Boston and New York in 1947, for the last time in 1976. It may

1984 Anne Margaret & Street   TV drama

be that the reason why *A Streetcar Named Desire* has not been staged for some twenty odd years is Tennessee Williams's ambivalent attitude to homosexuality (see Historical Background), unacceptable now that the issue of gay rights is no longer a debatable point. It might be added here as an ironical footnote that one of the most successful plays on Broadway in recent years was Tony Kushner's two-part epic of homosexuality, *Angels in America* (Part I, 1992; Part II, 1994).

PART SEVEN

B ROADER PERSPECTIVES

F URTHER READING

BIOGRAPHIES

A number of biographies of Tennessee Williams have been published, but most of them are of little interest except to those who are eager to learn more about his drug-taking and his homosexual affairs. There are, however, a few exceptions:

Ronald Hayman, *Tennessee Williams: Everyone Else is an Audience*, Yale University Press, New York and London, 1985

> A well-written biography with interesting quotations from Tennessee Williams and his friends

Donald Spoto, *The Kindness of Strangers: The Life of Tennessee Williams*, Bodley Head, 1985

> Crammed with facts yet surprisingly readable

Edwina Dakin Williams, *Remember Me to Tom*, G.P. Putnam's Sons, 1963; Cassell, 1964

> Mrs Williams's memories, ghosted by Lucy Freeman. Pedestrian in style but interesting, not least for what Mrs Williams has omitted to mention

Donald Windham, *Tennessee Williams' Letters to Donald Windham, 1940–65*, Holt, Rinehart & Winston, 1977

> Of literary as well as personal interest

LITERARY CRITICISM

There have been very few works of literary criticism on Tennessee Williams. Evidently his private life is deemed of more interest. A few might be mentioned here:

Catherine M. Arnott, (compiler), *Tennessee Williams on File* (Writers on File Series), Methuen, 1985

> A brief useful work which deals with his main plays and includes also extracts from reviews

Signi Falk, *Tennessee Williams*, Twayne Publishers, 1961
> A discussion of Tennessee Williams's plays, with too much emphasis on summaries of the plots

Nancy M. Tischler, *Tennessee Williams: Rebellious Puritan*, The Citadel Press, 1961
> A biography focusing on his work

The reader might well ask why so little has been published on Tennessee Williams as a writer, and also why hardly any of his plays have been revived since his death.

Neither question is easy to answer. Perhaps his private life proved too fascinating a subject for works of literary criticism to compete with?

There is no straightforward answer to the question of why his plays have so rarely been performed since his death. It may be that the gay lobby, powerful in the United States in particular, has understandably taken exception to Tennessee Williams's implicit condemnation of homosexuality.

Or perhaps it is simply that as a dramatist Tennessee Williams now belongs to the past: present-day American playwrights (like David Mamet, Arthur Kopit or Sam Shepherd) may imply that life is a farce, but they still take a moral stand. In Tennessee Williams's plays neither morality nor humour plays any significant part.

World events	1939	Arts	Tennessee Williams
Outbreak of Second World War in Europe		Film version of Margaret Mitchell's *Gone with the Wind*, starring Clark Gable and Vivien Leigh Film *The Wizard of Oz*, starring Judy Garland Publication of the novel *The Grapes of Wrath* by John Steinbeck	*American Blues*, a collection of three short plays by Tennessee Williams wins a prize at the Group Theatre Play Contest
Battle of Britain	1940	*The Long Mirror* by J.B. Priestley is staged Charlie Chaplin directs and stars in the film *The Great Dictator* Publication of the novel *For Whom the Bell Tolls* by Ernest Hemingway	The play *Battle of Angels* is not a success
USA joins the Allies against the Axis powers in the Second World War	1941	Orson Welles directs and stars in the film *Citizen Kane* Noel Coward's play *Blithe Spirit* is staged The play *Long Day's Journey into Night* by Eugene O'Neill is written	

World events		Arts	Tennessee Williams
	1942		
US naval-air victory at Midway Island ends Japanese expansion in the Pacific		Edward Hopper paints *Nighthawks* Publication of the novel *L'Etranger* by Albert Camus	
	1943		
British and American troops land at Salerno (*Stanley a Mitch*)		The Rodgers and Hammerstein musical *Oklahoma* is staged Jean-Paul Sartre's essay *Being and Nothingness* is published	Obtains a contract as a scriptwriter for MGM
	1944		
D-Day allied landings in Normandy		Laurence Olivier directs and stars in the film *Henry V* Bartok's Violin Concerto Jean-Paul Sartre's play *Huis Clos* is staged	The play *The Glass Menagerie* is staged
	1945		
US President Franklin D. Roosevelt dies. He is succeeded by Harry S. Truman American aircraft drops atomic bombs on Hiroshima and Nagasaki End of Second World War		The play *An Inspector Calls* by J.B. Priestley is staged George Orwell's novel *Animal Farm* is published	Starts work on the play *A Streetcar Named Desire* *Interesting comparisons can be made between the 3 texts.*

World events		Arts	Tennessee Williams
	1946		
An upsurge of labour unrest cripples large sections of US industry		The play *The Iceman Cometh* by Eugene O'Neill is staged	
		Publication of *A History of Western Philosophy* by Bertrand Russell	
		Publication of the poetry collection *North and South* by Elizabeth Bishop	
	1947		
India and Pakistan become independent		Arthur Miller's play *All My Sons* is staged	*A Streetcar Named Desire* is staged
		The Linden Tree by J.B. Priestley is staged	
		Henri Cartier-Bresson holds one-man show at New York's Museum of Modern Art	
	1948		
Britain, USA and France cooperate in establishing an airlift to West Berlin		The play *The Browning Version* by Terence Rattigan is staged	
Gandhi assassinated in Delhi		Swiss sculptor Alberto Giacometti has a successful exhibition in New York	
		Laurence Olivier directs and stars in the film *Hamlet*	
		The novel *La Peste* by Albert Camus is published	

World events		Arts	Tennessee Williams
	1949		
Chinese Communist People's Republic is proclaimed		The essay *The Second Sex* by Simone de Beauvoir is published	British première of *A Streetcar Named Desire* at the Aldwych Theatre, London, directed by Laurence Olivier
		Film *The Third Man* by Orson Welles is screened	*Again - possible to make some illuminating comparisons.*
		Arthur Miller's play *Death of a Salesman* is staged	
	1950		
General MacArthur, commanding the UN forces, launches a counter-offensive against the North Korean invaders in the Korean War		Commercial colour television broadcasting begins in the USA	*A Streetcar Named Desire* is staged in Paris, France
		Robert Doisneau produces the photograph *The Kiss* for *Life* magazine	Publication of *The Roman Spring of Mrs Stone*, a novel
	1951		
USA explodes the first hydrogen bomb		The film *The African Queen*, starring Humphrey Bogart and Audrey Hepburn, is screened	*A Streetcar Named Desire* is filmed, directed by Elia Kazan
			The Rose Tattoo is staged
		The novel *The Catcher in the Rye* by J.D. Salinger is published	*"phoney - quality"* *Comparison*

Bogart beat Brando for the Oscar - unfortunate coincidence of date

authorial voice the author, as distinct from the characters he has created, speaking directly to the readers

closet drama a play written to be read, not acted on the stage

coda in music a concluding passage which provides a satisfying ending. It is now also used of a literary work

coup de théâtre (French) a sudden startling turn of events in a play

deus ex machina (Latin) originally an actor playing a god brought on the stage by a mechanical device. Used to describe a contrived and unconvincing twist in a plot, as a way out of a difficulty

Expressionist presenting a distorted, exaggerated form of reality. The Expressionist movement started in Germany in the early twentieth century, and exercised a considerable influence on drama and film as well as on literature

figurative language language enriched by figures of speech such as metaphor

hubris (Greek) the overweening pride that is the cause of the downfall of a tragic hero

imagery the use of images, words that appeal to the emotions and senses, in a literary work

leitmotiv (German) recurring main theme (a borrowing from musical terminology)

metaphor figure of speech in which an object is spoken of as the thing it resembles in some way

simile comparison of a thing to another, on the basis of a shared quality. The word 'as' or 'like' always appears

symbolism the use of words to represent something else. The Symbolist movement in nineteenth-century literature believed in hidden meanings underlying reality

tableau vivant a living picture, a group of silent motionless actors representing a dramatic event

trope any figure of speech in which a word is used to represent something else (a metaphor or a simile is a trope)

unities the rules demanding unity of time, place and action in a play. These rules came to be ascribed to the Greek critic and philosopher Aristotle, and were regarded as imperative for the construction of a drama by literary theorists from the sixteenth to the nineteenth century

Hana Sambrook was educated at the Charles University in Prague and at the University of Edinburgh. She worked for some years as an editor in Scottish educational publishing, and was later on the staff of the Edinburgh University Library. Now a freelance editor in London, she is the author of several York Notes, including Sylvia Plath's *Selected Works* and *The Poetry of the First World War*.

Notes

NOTES

NOTES

Notes

Notes

Notes

Notes

Notes

NOTES

NOTES

York Notes Advanced (£3.99 each)

Margaret Atwood
The Handmaid's Tale

Jane Austen
Mansfield Park

Jane Austen
Persuasion

Jane Austen
Pride and Prejudice

Alan Bennett
Talking Heads

William Blake
Songs of Innocence and of Experience

Charlotte Brontë
Jane Eyre

Emily Brontë
Wuthering Heights

Geoffrey Chaucer
The Franklin's Tale

Geoffrey Chaucer
General Prologue to the Canterbury Tales

Geoffrey Chaucer
The Wife of Bath's Prologue and Tale

Joseph Conrad
Heart of Darkness

Charles Dickens
Great Expectations

John Donne
Selected Poems

George Eliot
The Mill on the Floss

F. Scott Fitzgerald
The Great Gatsby

E.M. Forster
A Passage to India

Brian Friel
Translations

Thomas Hardy
The Mayor of Casterbridge

Thomas Hardy
Tess of the d'Urbervilles

Seamus Heaney
Selected Poems from Opened Ground

Nathaniel Hawthorne
The Scarlet Letter

James Joyce
Dubliners

John Keats
Selected Poems

Christopher Marlowe
Doctor Faustus

Arthur Miller
Death of a Salesman

Toni Morrison
Beloved

William Shakespeare
Antony and Cleopatra

William Shakespeare
As You Like It

William Shakespeare
Hamlet

William Shakespeare
King Lear

William Shakespeare
Measure for Measure

William Shakespeare
The Merchant of Venice

William Shakespeare
Much Ado About Nothing

William Shakespeare
Othello

William Shakespeare
Romeo and Juliet

William Shakespeare
The Tempest

William Shakespeare
The Winter's Tale

Mary Shelley
Frankenstein

Alice Walker
The Color Purple

Oscar Wilde
The Importance of Being Earnest

Tennessee Williams
A Streetcar Named Desire

John Webster
The Duchess of Malfi

W.B. Yeats
Selected Poems

OTHER TITLES

GCSE and equivalent levels (£3.50 each)

Maya Angelou
I Know Why the Caged Bird Sings

Jane Austen
Pride and Prejudice

Alan Ayckbourn
Absent Friends

Elizabeth Barrett Browning
Selected Poems

Robert Bolt
A Man for All Seasons

Harold Brighouse
Hobson's Choice

Charlotte Brontë
Jane Eyre

Emily Brontë
Wuthering Heights

Shelagh Delaney
A Taste of Honey

Charles Dickens
David Copperfield

Charles Dickens
Great Expectations

Charles Dickens
Hard Times

Charles Dickens
Oliver Twist

Roddy Doyle
Paddy Clarke Ha Ha Ha

George Eliot
Silas Marner

George Eliot
The Mill on the Floss

William Golding
Lord of the Flies

Oliver Goldsmith
She Stoops To Conquer

Willis Hall
The Long and the Short and the Tall

Thomas Hardy
Far from the Madding Crowd

Thomas Hardy
The Mayor of Casterbridge

Thomas Hardy
Tess of the d'Urbervilles

Thomas Hardy
The Withered Arm and other Wessex Tales

L.P. Hartley
The Go-Between

Seamus Heaney
Selected Poems

Susan Hill
I'm the King of the Castle

Barry Hines
A Kestrel for a Knave

Louise Lawrence
Children of the Dust

Harper Lee
To Kill a Mockingbird

Laurie Lee
Cider with Rosie

Arthur Miller
The Crucible

Arthur Miller
A View from the Bridge

Robert O'Brien
Z for Zachariah

Frank O'Connor
My Oedipus Complex and other stories

George Orwell
Animal Farm

J.B. Priestley
An Inspector Calls

Willy Russell
Educating Rita

Willy Russell
Our Day Out

J.D. Salinger
The Catcher in the Rye

William Shakespeare
Henry IV Part 1

William Shakespeare
Henry V

William Shakespeare
Julius Caesar

William Shakespeare
Macbeth

William Shakespeare
The Merchant of Venice

William Shakespeare
A Midsummer Night's Dream

William Shakespeare
Much Ado About Nothing

William Shakespeare
Romeo and Juliet

William Shakespeare
The Tempest

William Shakespeare
Twelfth Night

George Bernard Shaw
Pygmalion

Mary Shelley
Frankenstein

R.C. Sherriff
Journey's End

Rukshana Smith
Salt on the snow

John Steinbeck
Of Mice and Men

Robert Louis Stevenson
Dr Jekyll and Mr Hyde

Jonathan Swift
Gulliver's Travels

Robert Swindells
Daz 4 Zoe

Mildred D. Taylor
Roll of Thunder, Hear My Cry

Mark Twain
Huckleberry Finn

James Watson
Talking in Whispers

William Wordsworth
Selected Poems

A Choice of Poets

Mystery Stories of the Nineteenth Century including The Signalman

Nineteenth Century Short Stories

Poetry of the First World War

Six Women Poets

Chinua Achebe
Things Fall Apart

Edward Albee
Who's Afraid of Virginia Woolf?

Margaret Atwood
Cat's Eye

Jane Austen
Emma

Jane Austen
Northanger Abbey

Jane Austen
Sense and Sensibility

Samuel Beckett
Waiting for Godot

Robert Browning
Selected Poems

Robert Burns
Selected Poems

Angela Carter
Nights at the Circus

Geoffrey Chaucer
The Merchant's Tale

Geoffrey Chaucer
The Miller's Tale

Geoffrey Chaucer
The Nun's Priest's Tale

Samuel Taylor Coleridge
Selected Poems

Daniel Defoe
Moll Flanders

Daniel Defoe
Robinson Crusoe

Charles Dickens
Bleak House

Charles Dickens
Hard Times

Emily Dickinson
Selected Poems

Carol Ann Duffy
Selected Poems

George Eliot
Middlemarch

T.S. Eliot
The Waste Land

T.S. Eliot
Selected Poems

Henry Fielding
Joseph Andrews

E.M. Forster
Howards End

John Fowles
The French Lieutenant's Woman

Robert Frost
Selected Poems

Elizabeth Gaskell
North and South

Stella Gibbons
Cold Comfort Farm

Graham Greene
Brighton Rock

Thomas Hardy
Jude the Obscure

Thomas Hardy
Selected Poems

Joseph Heller
Catch-22

Homer
The Iliad

Homer
The Odyssey

Gerard Manley Hopkins
Selected Poems

Aldous Huxley
Brave New World

Kazuo Ishiguro
The Remains of the Day

Ben Jonson
The Alchemist

Ben Jonson
Volpone

James Joyce
A Portrait of the Artist as a Young Man

Philip Larkin
Selected Poems

D.H. Lawrence
The Rainbow

D.H. Lawrence
Selected Stories

D.H. Lawrence
Sons and Lovers

D.H. Lawrence
Women in Love

John Milton
Paradise Lost Bks I & II

John Milton
Paradise Lost Bks IV & IX

Thomas More
Utopia

Sean O'Casey
Juno and the Paycock

George Orwell
Nineteen Eighty-four

John Osborne
Look Back in Anger

Wilfred Owen
Selected Poems

Sylvia Plath
Selected Poems

Alexander Pope
Rape of the Lock and other poems

Ruth Prawer Jhabvala
Heat and Dust

Jean Rhys
Wide Sargasso Sea

William Shakespeare
As You Like It

William Shakespeare
Coriolanus

William Shakespeare
Henry IV Pt 1

William Shakespeare
Henry V

William Shakespeare
Julius Caesar

William Shakespeare
Macbeth

William Shakespeare
Measure for Measure

William Shakespeare
A Midsummer Night's Dream

William Shakespeare
Richard II

William Shakespeare
Richard III

William Shakespeare
Sonnets

William Shakespeare
The Taming of the Shrew

William Shakespeare
Twelfth Night

William Shakespeare
The Winter's Tale

George Bernard Shaw
Arms and the Man

George Bernard Shaw
Saint Joan

Muriel Spark
The Prime of Miss Jean Brodie

John Steinbeck
The Grapes of Wrath

John Steinbeck
The Pearl

Tom Stoppard
Arcadia

Tom Stoppard
Rosencrantz and Guildenstern are Dead

Jonathan Swift
Gulliver's Travels and The Modest Proposal

Alfred, Lord Tennyson
Selected Poems

W.M. Thackeray
Vanity Fair

Virgil
The Aeneid

Edith Wharton
The Age of Innocence

Tennessee Williams
Cat on a Hot Tin Roof

Tennessee Williams
The Glass Menagerie

Virginia Woolf
Mrs Dalloway

Virginia Woolf
To the Lighthouse

William Wordsworth
Selected Poems

Metaphysical Poets

York Notes – the Ultimate Literature Guides

York Notes are recognised as the best literature study guides.
If you have enjoyed using this book and have found it useful, you
can now order others directly from us – simply follow the ordering
instructions below.

HOW TO ORDER

Decide which title(s) you require and then order in one of the following
ways:

Booksellers
All titles available from good bookstores.

By post
List the title(s) you require in the space provided overleaf,
select your method of payment, complete your name and
address details and return your completed order form and
payment to:

> *Addison Wesley Longman Ltd*
> *PO BOX 88*
> *Harlow*
> *Essex CM19 5SR*

By phone
Call our Customer Information Centre on 01279 623923 to
place your order, quoting mail number: HEYN1.

By fax
Complete the order form overleaf, ensuring you fill in your
name and address details and method of payment, and fax it
to us on 01279 414130.

By e-mail
E-mail your order to us on awlhe.orders@awl.co.uk listing
title(s) and quantity required and providing full name and
address details as requested overleaf. Please quote mail
number: HEYN1. Please do not send credit card details by
e-mail.

York Notes Order Form

Titles required:

Quantity	Title/ISBN	Price

Sub total _____

Please add £2.50 postage & packing _____

(*P & P is free for orders over £50*) _____

Total _____

Mail no: HEYN1

Your Name _____

Your Address _____

_____

Postcode _____ Telephone _____

Method of payment

☐ I enclose a cheque or a P/O for £_____ made payable to Addison Wesley Longman Ltd

☐ Please charge my Visa/Access/AMEX/Diners Club card
Number _____ Expiry Date _____
Signature _____ Date _____

(please ensure that the address given above is the same as for your credit card)

Prices and other details are correct at time of going to press but may change without notice. All orders are subject to status.

☐ *Please tick this box if you would like a complete listing of Longman Study Guides (suitable for GCSE and A-level students)*

◉ York Press

▣ Longman

Addison Wesley Longman